HEINZ
GUDERIAN

LEADERSHIP ■ STRATEGY ■ CONFLICT

PIER P. BATTI   ADAM HOOK

First published in Great Britain in 2011 by Osprey Publishing,
Midland House, West Way, Botley, Oxford OX2 0PH, UK
44-02 23rd St, Suite 219, Long Island City, NY 11101, USA

E-mail: info@ospreypublishing.com

A CIP catalogue record for this book is available from the British Library.

ISBN: 978 1 84908 366 9
E-book ISBN: 978 1 84908 367 6

Editorial by Ilios Publishing Ltd, Oxford, UK (www.iliospublishing.com)
Page layout by Myriam Bell Design
Index by Sandra Shotter
Typeset in 1Stone Serif and Officina Sans
Maps by Mapping Specialists Ltd
Originated by PPS Grasmere Ltd
Printed in China through Worldprint Ltd

11 12 13 14 15   10 9 8 7 6 5 4 3 2 1

www.ospreypublishing.com

Artist's note

Readers may care to note that the original paintings from which the
colour plates in this book were prepared are available for private sale. The
Publishers retain all reproduction copyright whatsoever. All enquiries
should be addressed to:

Scorpio Gallery, PO Box 475, Hailsham, East Sussex, BN27 2SL, UK

The Publishers regret that they can enter into no correspondence upon
this matter.

Table of ranks

German	British	USA
Leutnant	Second Lieutenant	Second Lieutenant
Oberleutnant	Lieutenant	First Lieutenant
Hauptmann	Captain	Captain
Major	Major	Major
Oberstleutnant	Lieutenant-Colonel	Lieutenant-Colonel
Oberst	Colonel	Colonel Brigadier*
Generalmajor	Brigadier*	Brigadier-General
Generalleutnant	Major-General	Major-General
General der...**	Lieutenant-General	Lieutenant-General
Generaloberst	General	General
Generalfeldmarschall	Field Marshal	General of the Army

Notes:
* equivalent to *Generalmajor* and brigadier-general, but not a general rank
**rank completed with the arm of service or speciality of the owner

The Woodland Trust

Osprey Publishing are supporting the Woodland Trust, the UK's leading
woodland conservation charity, by funding the dedication of trees.

Front cover: The Tank Museum, 3222A5

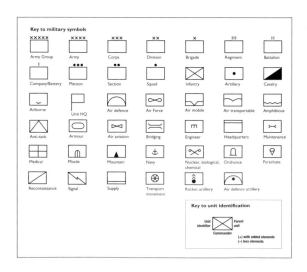

CONTENTS

INTRODUCTION

Guderian is presented with a French flag captured at Juniville by Oberstleutnant Hermann Balck, commander of Schützen-Regiment 1. This photo was taken at La Neuville on 11 June 1940. (IWM, MH 10935)

'Panzer General' is an epithet that can be applied easily to Heinz Guderian given his role in the development of armoured warfare. He was the creator of the German armoured force, the one he successfully led on the battlefield against Poland in 1939 and then against France in 1940. From this point of view Guderian's career is unique; unlike other military innovators throughout the world, he successfully had a voice in the development of new doctrines and tactics which (quite exceptionally again) he tested first-hand on the battlefield, with highly remarkable results. As such Guderian is revealed not only a valid theoretician, but also a first-class field commander. He was also lucky in that he avoided, unlike other legendary field commanders, eventual failure and defeat on the battlefield. Even though Operation *Barbarossa*, the German attack against the Soviet Union, failed in the end, Guderian is not associated with that failure but instead his record as a field commander up to December 1941, when he was removed from command of 2. Panzerarmee, emphasizes his command and leadership qualities. The fact that his removal prevented him from facing the first defeat on the battlefield suffered by the German Army in World War II certainly helped his reputation. If Guderian's military career had ended here then perhaps an enduring myth might have developed. However, it did not and eventually Guderian returned to a familiar role: that of a staff officer, not so different from the many other staff officers in the German army.

This is actually closer to the truth about Guderian than that of the battlefield Panzer leader. Guderian was very much a product of the German staff tradition. He was a fringe member of the Prussian military elite, and took part in World War I without seeing a great deal of service on the battlefield.

His return to national service brought him back into this staff environment, first as Generalinspekteur der Panzertruppen (Inspector of the Panzer Troops) and eventually, following the failed attempt on Hitler's life, as Chef des Stabes des Oberkommando des Heeres) (Chief of Army Staff).

These were both aspirational appointments for a German general, but not ones likely to ensure long-term stardom, particularly as Guderian's role on the Eastern Front does not necessarily stand up to deep scrutiny. However, Guderian's reputation has prospered in the post-war years largely owing to his remarkable, and largely underrated, writing skills. Guderian's post-war memoirs – *Panzer Leader* – became, like his earlier book *Achtung – Panzer!*, a stunning literary and commercial success that is still read, analyzed and criticized by both enthusiasts and scholars nearly 60 years after its first publication.

Just as *Achtung – Panzer!* brought him to the limelight as an innovator before World War II, his memoirs brought him back to public attention and eventually contributed to the creation of the myth of the 'Panzer General' that endures to this day. These publications portray Guderian successfully as the 'father' of the German Panzer arm, both during the pre-war period and the early blitzkrieg years, while avoiding any focus on his later activities as Generalinspekteur der Panzertruppen and Chef des Stabes des OKH, as well as his close relationship with Hitler. It is these writings that have largely dominated the historical debates around Guderian's role in the Nazi regime and his battlefield successes, ensuring that his own perspective of events has largely held centre stage.

A portrait of Heinz Guderian after he had been awarded the Ritterkreuz (Knight's Cross) on 27 October 1939 while commanding XIX AK (mot.) during the Polish campaign. (IWM, HU 2410)

EARLY YEARS

Heinz Wilhelm Guderian was born on 17 June 1888 at Kulm (modern Chelmno) on the Vistula, in a part of Eastern Prussia that became part of Poland following the end of World War I. Guderian's family (both on the paternal and the maternal side) were landowners and, to a lesser extent, soldiers. At the time of his birth Guderian's father, Friedrich, was a regular soldier holding the rank of *Oberleutnant* in the German army (he would rise to the rank of *General der Infanterie*). This would prove a great influence on both Heinz and his brother, and from the age of 13 he had decided to become an army officer. After attending school at Colmar, in Alsace, on 1 April 1901 Heinz and his younger brother Fritz went to Karlsruhe, in the region of Baden, to attend the cadet school – a preparatory school for the would-be officers. Transferring to the main cadet school at Gross-Lichterfelde, near Berlin, on

1 February 1903, Guderian graduated in February 1907 and immediately entered the army on 28 February 1907 as a *Fahnenjunker* (officer candidate) in 10. Jäger-Bataillon at Bitche, also in Alsace. Whether a coincidence or not, this was Heinz's father's command until December 1908, which certainly helped his early career. After the compulsory course taken at the Kriegsschule (War School) in Metz between 10 April and 14 December 1907, Heinz was promoted *Leutnant* (second lieutenant) on 27 January 1908, his seniority backdated to

22 June 1906. On 1 October 1909 Guderian was sent, along with the entire 10. Jäger-Bataillon, to Goslar and three years later, on 1 October 1912, he was detached to the 3. Telegraphen-Bataillon in Coblenz. This, and the subsequent detachment to the Kriegsakademie (War Academy) in Berlin on 1 October 1913, would influence Guderian's military career by giving him a technical background. On 1 October 1913 Heinz Guderian also married Margarete Goerne, the daughter of a medical general officer. They had two sons, Heinz Günter (born 23 August 1914) and Kurt (born 17 September 1917).

With the outbreak of the World War I in August 1914 Guderian became commander of Funk Station (heavy radio station) 3 and Nachrichten Offizier (communication officer) of 5. Kavallerie-Division, engaged on the Western Front. This lasted until 4 October of the same year when Guderian took over command of the Funk Station 13, thus becoming Nachrichten Offizier on the staff of AOK (Armeeoberkommando) 4. On 8 November he was promoted *Oberleutnant*. In this role, between May 1915 and January 1916, Guderian was also an auxiliary officer in charge of the signal intelligence of AOK 4, a role he also carried out at the HQ of the AOK 5 when he was transferred there on 27 January 1916, before going back to AOK 4 on 18 July following battlefield experience at Verdun. During this period Guderian was promoted *Hauptmann* on 15 November 1915. On 3 April 1917 Guderian's career took a diversion when he became quartermaster officer, first with the staff of 4. Infanterie-Division, then (from April to May) with the staff of AOK 1, then (from May to June) with the staff of the 52. Reserve-Division during the battle of the Aisne, and finally (from June to July) to the staff of the Gardekorps. Between July and August 1917 Guderian was intelligence officer with the staff of X Reservekorps, before being moved to the staff of 4. Infanterie-Division until 11 August 1917. In September he became commander of II. Bataillon of Infanterie-Regiment 14, a position he held until 24 October 1917 when he became operations officer (Ia) with the staff of the AOK C; during this period he was detached to the sixth Lehrgang für Generalstabsoffiziere (general staff course) at Sedan, which lasted for one month (10 January–8 February 1918); on 27 February 1918 Guderian was detached to the Generalstab der Armee (Army General Staff) before returning as a quartermaster officer with the staff of the XXXVIII Reservekorps on 23 May 1918. On 20 September he took over the role of operations officer with the staff of the German representative in occupied Italy, a position he held until the end of the war there on 8 November 1918.

In November 1918 Guderian held briefly two positions in the field and replacement army before being assigned to the command of the Zentralstelle Grenzschutz Ost (Border Protection East Central Office), a position that brought him to the War Ministry in Berlin. Between January and October 1919 Guderian served on the German eastern border, first with the border protection HQs at Breslau and Bartenstein, then with the staff of the Eiserne Division ('Iron Division') at Riga, before joining the Reichswehr on 30 October 1919 – one of 4,000 officers out of a 100,000-man army. First detached to Reichswehr-Brigade 10, on 16 January 1920 Guderian took over command of 3. Kompanie of 10. Jäger-Bataillon, which he led during the protests and riots in western and central Germany in 1920–21. Between May 1920 and January 1922 Guderian was also a company commander with 20. Reichswehr-Infanterie-Regiment and the III. Bataillon of 17. Infanterie-Regiment, until on 16 January 1922 he was detached to the 7. (Bayerische) Kraftfahr-Abteilung (Motor Transport Battalion) in Munich, which enabled him to gain some experience before joining the Abteilung für Kraftfahrtruppe (Department of Motor Transport Troops) at the Reichswehr Ministerium (RWM) at Berlin on 1 April 1922.

This department was in charge of studying and developing the motorization of the army, which at the time mainly meant motor transport of troops and supplies, since the development of armoured fighting vehicles was forbidden by the Versailles peace treaty. Guderian was a perfect fit for this position given his experience as a staff officer covering areas such as operations, quartermaster and communications/intelligence, though, like many other officers at this time, he was completely unfamiliar with the field of motorization. Guderian was at the RWM until 1 October 1924, when he became an instructor with the staff of the 2. Division at Stettin, before returning to the RWM, this time to the transport office of the operations department, on 1 October 1927. Promoted *Major* on 1 February 1927, he worked at the RWM until 1 October 1928, when he was detached to the Kraftfahrlehrstab (Motor Transport Instruction Staff) in Berlin to teach about tank tactics. He left this position and the RWM on 1 February 1930, when he took over command of the 3. Preussische Kraftfahr-Abteilung (Motor Transport Battalion) with a promotion to *Oberstleutnant*. On 1 October 1931 Guderian was back at the RWM, this time as chief of staff of the Inspector of Motor Transport Troops, one Oswald Lutz.

A smiling Guderian. In spite of how he appeared on photos and in newsreels, Guderian was a far from calm and joyful man. His scratchy personality and his bursts of rage earned him the nickname 'Heinz Brausewetter', 'Heinz stormy weather'. (IWM, MH 9404)

MILITARY LIFE

The evolution of the office of the Inspector of Motor Transport Troops is revealing of the change in its duties; when appointed in April 1931 Lutz was just inspector, but on 1 July 1934 he also became commander of the motor troops following the creation of the Kommando der Kraftfahrtruppen (Motor Transport Troops Command). On 15 October 1935, following the German rearmament, Lutz became Inspector of Kraftfahrkampftruppen und Heeresmotorisierung (Combat Motor Transport Troops and Army Motorization) and was promoted *General der Panzertruppen* – the first commander of the Panzer troops, a position he held until 15 February 1936. Guderian was Chief of Staff of the inspection until 1 July 1934, when – following his promotion to *Oberst* on 1 October 1933 – he became Chief of Staff of the Kommando der Kraftfahrtruppen until 15 October 1935, when he took over command of the newly formed 2. Panzer-Division in Würzburg. First promoted *Generalmajor* on 1 August 1936 and then *Generalleutnant* on 10 February of the same year, on 4 February 1938 Guderian took over the post of commander of the Panzertruppen directly from Lutz. The evolution of this command also gave Guderian control of XVI Armeekorps (the army's first Panzer corps) on 1 April, and from 24 November 1938 – one day after his promotion to *General der Panzertruppen* – also the title of Chief of the Schnelle Truppen, the 'fast troops' now encompassing all the armoured and motorized units.

The waltz of positions and appointments simply reveals how quick the development of the Panzertruppen was from a simple idea on paper to deployable combat formations. On 1 October 1934, following Lutz's appointment as commander of Kraftfahrtruppen, the 1. Panzer-Brigade was secretly formed in Germany with two Panzer regiments, which existed predominantly on paper. One year later, on 15 October 1935 (the date of official creation of the Panzertruppen), the first three Panzer divisions were created, each with a Panzer regiment. At this stage the commander of the Panzertruppen was only responsible for tank units, while the Chief of the schnelle Truppen was also responsible for all other units that actually formed part of the Panzer divisions: motorized infantry, artillery, anti-tank, reconnaissance and even cavalry, along with their schools and replacement units. The creation of XVI AK added further responsibilities for the commander of the Panzertruppen/schnelle Truppen. So while Guderian, who held both positions, was

On 22 September 1939 a parade was held at Brest-Litovsk to celebrate the handing over of the city to the Soviet Union. To Guderian's right is General Viktorin, commander of 20. Infanterie-Division (mot.), to his left the Soviet General Kriwoschein.
(IWM, HU 85899)

previously largely committed to theoretical training and unit organization, the corps command gave him direct operational control of the first three Panzer divisions formed, which were then grouped under the first 'motorized' corps.

On 10 March 1938 the Panzertruppen had their first test when 2. Panzer Division spearheaded the German troops (under XVI AK's command) in the annexation of Austria. Led by Guderian, the division performed more than satisfactorily, covering 690km (420 miles) in two days, albeit at the cost of 30 per cent of its tanks due to breakdowns and accidents. Guderian also led the peaceful seizure of the Sudetenland that started on 2 October 1938, this time at a much slower pace. Following mobilization of the German army in preparation for the campaign against Poland, on 26 August 1939 Guderian left both his assignments as Chief of the Schnelle Truppen and commander of XVI AK to take over command of the newly formed XIX AK (mot.), made of one Panzer and two motorized

At 0800hrs on 12 May 1940 1. Panzer-Division, leading the advance of Guderian's XIX AK (mot.) across the Ardennes, seized Bouillon, the last Belgian town before Sedan, which became Guderian's HQ for a few days. Here he watches the rebuilding of the bridge on the Semois River along with his aide, Oberstleutnant Riebel. (IWM, MH 9405)

infantry divisions. Guderian led the corps during the campaign against Poland until the end of September, when it was brought back to Germany for rest and refit. The Polish campaign earned Guderian his Ritterkreuz (Knight's Cross), which was awarded to him on 27 October 1939 once his World War I Iron Crosses first and second class had been upgraded.

In February 1940 XIX AK (mot.) was reorganized. Now with three Panzer divisions it was placed under the command of Panzergruppe von Kleist along with Hermann Hoth's XV AK, which had two other Panzer divisions. As such, Panzergruppe von Kleist controlled half of the German Panzer force, now consisting of ten divisions following the reorganization of four 'light' divisions into Panzer divisions and the forming of the tenth one. Although not the most experienced commander, Guderian was given the most important task of the entire campaign – the crossing of the Meuse at Sedan, establishment of a bridgehead and advance west towards the Channel. After a fast drive across the Ardennes from 10 May 1940 onwards, Guderian's XIX AK (mot.) established its bridgehead on the Meuse on the 13th and two days later started its drive west to the Channel, which it reached on 20 May. Only briefly engaged against the Dunkirk pocket, XIX AK (mot.) was withdrawn from the front and reorganized for the second part of the campaign against France, Fall *Rot*. On 1 June 1940 the unit was renamed Panzergruppe Guderian, and now had XXXIX and XXXXI AK (mot.) under command. Panzergruppe Guderian was now made up of four Panzer and two motorized infantry divisions. It started the attack against the Weygand Line (the French defence line running along the Aisne–Somme rivers) on 9 June 1940, and after a swift advance reached the Swiss border on 17 June completely surrounding the remnants of three French armies and the entire Maginot Line defences. On the

A well-known photograph of Guderian inside his SdKfz 251/6 command half-track during the campaign in the West, May–June 1940. The vehicle belonged to Korps Nachrichten Abteilung (mot.) (motorized corps communication unit) 80, which was attached to the staff of XIX AK (mot.). Originally consisting of two companies, it was expanded to four at the end of 1939. This unit was subsequently attached to the staff of Panzergruppe 2 and became a regiment in December 1940. (IWM, MH 29100)

22nd France signed an armistice with Germany, and at the end of the month Panzergruppe Guderian was disbanded, reverting to its original designation. On 19 July 1940 Heinz Guderian was promoted *Generaloberst*, one of the many promotions that followed the German victory in the West.

During the following months Guderian spent his time reorganizing the units under his command and studying the lessons of the French campaign. On 16 November 1940 XIX AK (mot.) was expanded and renamed again, this time permanently. Guderian became commander of the newly formed Panzergruppe 2, one of the four Panzer groups destined to take part in the campaign against the Soviet Union that started on 22 June 1940. Put under command of the Heeresgruppe Mitte along with Hoth's Panzergruppe 3, at the start of Operation *Barbarossa* Panzergruppe 2 consisted of three corps with a grand total of five Panzer divisions, three motorized infantry divisions (one of which of was Waffen-SS), one cavalry division and corps troops including Infanterie-Regiment 'Grossdeutschland' and Flak-Regiment 'Hermann Göring'. Panzergruppe 2 started its attack against the Soviet Union on 22 June by establishing bridgeheads across the Bug River; six days later its spearheads, advancing through the marshy Prjpet area, established a bridgehead on the Berezina River. From there the Panzergruppe advanced to the Dnieper, where a bridgehead was established on 10–11 July. Meanwhile, Panzergruppen 2 and 3 had also closed the Minsk pocket, with 300,000 Russians taken prisoner. The next step was the attack against Smolensk, which was completed by early August. Just before the end of the battle, on 28 July, Guderian's Panzergruppe 2 was upgraded and renamed Armeegruppe Guderian, a provisional army-level command (it reverted back to its status on 3 August). By the end of the battle for Smolensk another 300,000 Russian prisoners had been taken, along with 3,200 tanks and more than 3,000 guns. On 17 July 1941 Guderian was awarded the Eichenlaub (Oak Leaves) to his Ritterkreuz.

With his forces facing the Desna River, less than 300km (175 miles) from Moscow, the Soviet capital was, at least theoretically, within Panzergruppe 2's grasp, as in one and half months it had already advanced more than 650km (400 miles) into Soviet territory. However, following a decision by Hitler, Panzergruppe 2 moved south on 22–23 August 1941 to join up with Panzergruppe 1 and close a huge pocket around Kiev. On 15 September, after a 320km (200-mile) drive to the south, the vanguards of Panzergruppe 2 had established contact with Panzergruppe 1 at Lokhvitsa and closed the pocket. Four Soviet armies were encircled, and the battle of Kiev alone cost the Red Army a total of 660,000 men, some 880 tanks and 3,700 guns. Guderian and his Panzergruppe, which on 5 October 1941 was renamed 2. Panzerarmee, had little time to rest and refit. On 30 September the assault against Moscow, Operation *Typhoon*, was launched and it started well for Guderian's forces. They reached Orel on 3 October, and on the 7th the pincers closed around the Bryansk pocket, adding another 660,000 Soviet prisoners as well as 1,200 tanks and more than 5,000 guns. By mid-October a lack of supplies imposed a pause on operations, as did bad weather and stiffening Soviet resistance. Guderian's advance was resumed on 27 October, this time at a much slower pace. After the failure of an attempted *coup de main* against Tula on 29 October, by mid-November Guderian's forces were still around the city facing Soviet counterattacks. On 18 November 2. Panzerarmee started its final attack east of Tula and broke through as far as the Don River in spite of Soviet resistance and counterattacks. On 2–4 December the attempt to capture Tula failed and with it the assault on Moscow. On 4–5 December 1941, just before the

first Soviet major counteroffensive on the Eastern Front started, Guderian shifted 2. Panzerarmee to the defensive on his own initiative, and started to pull back from the most advanced, and threatened, positions.

Guderian only experienced the first phase of the Soviet counteroffensive. Confronted with a critical situation he adopted an elastic defence and withdrew from his forward positions, which displeased Hitler and eventually led to his removal from command of the 2. Panzerarmee on 26 December 1941. Put in the officers' reserve, Guderian's career seemed for many months to be at an end, since, in spite of the developments of the situation on the Eastern Front and in North Africa, he was not called back to active duty and rather, from 16 January 1942, was assigned to the staff of the replacement army corps stationed in Berlin. Only after the disaster of Stalingrad was Guderian considered for another appointment, though not for a field command. Recalled to duty on 28 February 1943, Guderian was given again a familiar role to play as he became the new Generalinspekteur der Panzertruppen. What may sound like a step back to 1935 was in fact a giant leap forward. The Panzertruppen were now in a pretty bad shape and a major reorganization was needed, a task Guderian undertook with unprecedented powers. Not directly involved in the Kursk offensive of July 1943, to which he was opposed, Guderian's major task in the latter half of 1943 and the first half of 1944 was the reorganization of the Panzer forces intended to oppose the Allied invasion in the West. It was shortly after this had taken place that Guderian became the new Chef des Stabes des Oberkommando des Heeres following the failed attempt to assassinate Hitler on 20 July 1944. As such he became directly involved in

Heinz Guderian during the early stages of Operation *Barbarossa*. Here he holds the rank of *Generaloberst*, to which he was promoted on 19 July 1940, and round his neck sports the Eichenlaub (Oakleaves) to the Ritterkreuz, awarded on 17 July 1941. This was the peak of his career. (IWM, AP 30928)

Guderian and his staff observing the early start of Operation *Typhoon*. The offensive against Moscow started at 0635hrs on 30 September 1941. Some two months later the offensive ended with the Soviet counterattack, and Guderian was relieved of his command.
(IWM, MH 9239)

the management of the war on the Eastern Front, while at the same time keeping his assignment as Generalinspekteur der Panzertruppen.

When he took over the new assignment, Guderian had to face the darkest hours of the German Army in the East. Following the Soviet offensive that started on 22 June 1944, Heeresgruppe Mitte had been destroyed, and in August the Red Army swept into the Balkans following the surrender, and the change of side, of Romania on 25 August and Bulgaria on 9 September 1944. At the end of 1944 the Red Army was pressing against the German border in East Prussia and stood at the gates of Warsaw and Budapest, directly threatening the core of the Reich. Guderian's assignment as Chef des Stabes des OKH did not survive the new offensive started by the Red Army on 17 January 1945, launched in part to relieve the pressure against the Allied forces in the Ardennes. On 28 March 1945, a few days after the Soviet drive north into Pomerania and East Prussia had started following the ill-fated German counteroffensive of 16–20 February, and after another clash with Hitler, Guderian was granted leave and, in practice, relieved of his assignment. Still Generalinspekteur der Panzertruppen, he joined his staff in the Tyrol where he eventually surrendered to American forces on 10 May 1945, being released from captivity on 16 June 1948. Retiring with his wife to Schwangau, in the Allgäu, Heinz Wilhelm Guderian died on 14 May 1954 and was buried in his beloved Goslar.

A successful writer

A fact often overlooked in Guderian's career is his success as a writer, which is closely related to the myth of his 'fatherhood' of the Panzertruppen. Guderian's first book, *Achtung – Panzer!*, written in the winter of 1936–37 on the suggestion of General Lutz, analyzed the evolution of the tank force, its tactics and its operational capabilities. Unlike other books on the subject, it was widely distributed and became known to the general public and even abroad. It was also reprinted in 1943 with the title *Die Panzerwaffe*. Even though this title brought fame to its author, Guderian's masterpiece was his memoirs, first published in Germany in 1950 with the title *Erinnerungen eines Soldaten*. Translated in English as *Panzer Leader* and published in the UK and the USA in 1952, it became the most widely read memoir of a German general, and it was subsequently translated and published in several other countries including Brazil, Argentina, France, Spain, Italy, Finland, Yugoslavia, Poland, Soviet Union and China. By the 1970s it had sold more than 180,000 copies all over the world. In 2003, it had reached its 18th printing in Germany alone.

HOUR OF DESTINY

The 'father' of the Panzertruppen

It is worth noting that the whole issue of Guderian's 'fatherhood' of the Panzertruppe is a direct consequence of the evolution of history writing during the last 50 years. When Guderian's memoirs were published in Germany in 1950, and translated in English two years later, they provided the only source on the early creation and subsequent development of the Panzertruppen at a time when the German records were still inaccessible. It is also important to remember that, until 1935, most of the activity related to the creation of the Panzertruppen was undertaken in secret, thus leaving few traces. It is therefore hardly surprising that history writers made use of Guderian's memoirs as the basis for these events, thus contributing to the birth of the myth of his 'fatherhood' of the Panzertruppen. What is a book of personal recollections and memoirs, and as such unavoidably self-centred (though Guderian certainly overplayed his own role in the early days of the Panzertruppen), became a historical source which, following new studies based on the actual records, history writers began to criticize, eventually questioning the Guderian myth and his pioneering role in the creation of the German armoured force.

When Guderian joined 7. Kraftfahr-Abteilung led by Major Lutz in January 1922, before joining Abteilung für Kraftfahrtruppe the following April, he had no technical background in either motorization or armoured warfare. Other officers in the Reichswehr possessed the necessary know-how and put it to good use. Leutnant Ernst Volckheim, who fought in a tank unit in 1918, joined the Abteilung für Kraftfahrtruppe in 1923 and two years later became instructor of armoured and motorized tactics at the infantry school in Döberitz. In 1923 and 1924 he published two books on armoured warfare, *Die deutsche Kampfwagen in Weltkrieg* and *Der Kampfwagen in der heutigen Kriegführung* (*German Combat Tanks in the World War* and *The Tank in Modern Warfare*), plus two-dozen articles in the semi-official army journal *Militär-Wochenblatt* (*Military Weekly Magazine*). Between 1922 and 1928 Guderian only wrote five articles that can be directly attributed to him, though the number may be higher, despite having acquired more experience. In the winter of 1923–24 he was given task of leading a wargame dealing with cooperation between motorized troops and air support by the then Major von Brauchitsch (later commander-in-chief of the German Army). His subsequent tour teaching tactics and military history to the staff of 2. Infanterie-Division clearly suggests that his superiors trusted his abilities, especially taking into account the fact

Guderian demonstrated the new Panzer formations – equipped with Panzer I tanks – for the first time in front of Hitler early in 1934. Hitler is supposed to have remarked 'This is what I need' and the first three new Panzer divisions were formed on 15 October 1935. (Carlo Pecchi)

that his commander at this point was the former Inspector of Motor Transport Troops, General Erich von Tschischwitz, who was himself a pioneer in the field. This is all in spite of the fact that Guderian only used a real tank for the first time in 1929, when on a tour of duty in Sweden. However, Guderian's willingness to learn and some kind of innate instinct brought him to the attention of his superiors and successfully launched his career. He was also

Since Germany could not have AFVs under the conditions of the Treaty of Versailles, troops were trained using the 'Attrappen', dummy tanks made of woods and mounted on every kind of vehicle. Note the use of mixed service and fatigue uniforms.
(Nik Cornish, WH 999)

helped by a successful series of manoeuvres held by the III. (Lehr) Bataillon of Infanterie-Regiment 9 at Spandau after Guderian had been appointed as a tactical instructor with the Kraftfahrlehrstab in Berlin. Using 'Attrappen', or wooden mock-ups of tanks mounted on cars or motorcycles, manoeuvres and exercises were held studying the employment of the Panzer as single vehicles, at platoon, company and battalion level.

In October 1926 Oberst Alfred von Vollard Bockelberg became Inspector of Motor Transport Troops, a dedicated man who believed in tanks and motorization, and it was under his supervision as chief of the army weapons department (Chef des Heeres Waffen Amts) that both the Panzer I and II – then officially designated 'agricultural tractors' – were developed in 1932–33. Oberst Oswald Lutz became his chief of staff, a position he maintained also under Bockelberg's successor, General Otto von Stülpnagel. No fan of tank warfare, on hearing of Guderian's exercises he prohibited any theoretical exercise with tanks above regimental level on the premise that 'the Panzer Divisions are a utopia'. In the autumn of 1929 Lutz got in touch again with Guderian and asked him to take over command of a motor transport battalion. On 1 April 1931 Lutz replaced Stülpnagel as inspector and asked Guderian to take on the duties of chief of staff, which he did from 1 October. The relationship between Lutz and Guderian is both hard to describe and to understand (it should be noted that Guderian wrote *Achtung – Panzer!* on Lutz's suggestion), particularly because the latter did not reserve much space in his memoirs to someone who has been described as his 'mentor'. Undoubtedly, theirs was a successful partnership that lasted throughout the decisive years of Hitler's rise to power and the start of the German rearmament. It would be wrong to split hairs on exactly who did what, especially as the Kommando der Kraftfahrtruppen also included other high-profile Panzer officers like Walther Nehring and Hermann Breith. One point should be highlighted though, and that is that it was thanks to Guderian, the former communication officer, that the highly effective communications system used by Panzer units was developed.

It is quite clear that Guderian was certainly not the first nor even the foremost 'Panzer pioneer', though he possessed the skills, capabilities and willingness to learn and to develop that characterize true pioneers. On the other hand, it must also be acknowledged that Guderian was to play a key role in the decisive moments of the development of the Panzertruppen. If it is true that he was not the key figure in the actual process, given the fact that a large group of German officers, at every level, believed in armoured warfare and were inclined towards the creation of Panzer units, the creation of the first Panzer divisions was only the first step in a long and complicated process. Confusion reigned over how these units were to be employed, at every level from battlefield tactics to operational manoeuvre. There were also technical problems, given the fast development of combat tanks and the gap between production and requirements. Until March 1938 the only actual battlefield experience gained by the Panzertruppen was their limited involvement in the Spanish Civil War, which saw personnel rotated through the only Panzer-Abteilung deployed between 1936 and 1939. If that helped crews to gain some actual combat experience at tactical level, the overall organization and doctrine of the Panzertruppen were still quite confused. In 1937 several new tank regiments and battalions were formed, a first step towards the expansion of the Panzertruppen also matched by the full motorization of four infantry divisions. However, in the meantime, following the French example of the division légère mécanique (light mechanized division), the decision was made to create four 'light' divisions (leichte Division) made of a mixture of cavalry and armour.

These steps were taking the Panzertruppen towards a completely different role than that envisaged by both Lutz and Guderian, who favoured concentration of forces, and of armour, in a few Panzer divisions that would play a decisive role in the battlefield. This led to excesses on both sides; Lutz and Guderian favoured the 'tank heavy' Panzer division with 480 or more tanks, which eventually led to the creation of the Panzer division with two Panzer regiments, an actual tank establishment in 1935 of 560 light tanks. This was no solution as there were no medium combat tanks able to face

Schützen, or motorized infantry, dismounting from an SdKfz 251/A half-track. Developed in 1937, this innovative vehicle enabled German infantry to keep up with the Panzers and approach the battle area under protection, a concept close to Guderian's heart. (Nik Cornish, WH 312)

During the last years of war the Panzer IV was the main battle tank of the Panzerwaffe. Although Guderian would have preferred to halt its production in early 1943 to concentrate on the Panther, it carried on until early 1945. A column of Panzer IV Ausf. Gs on the Eastern Front, 1943–44. (Nik Cornish, WH 767)

enemy tanks and anti-tank guns – the Panzerwaffe was not ready yet for the battlefield. Only in 1935 did the first German medium tank, the Panzer III, enter production and this was not without problems. Guderian wanted it armed with a 50mm gun instead of its 37mm one, but that gun did not yet exist and the upgrade took place only in late 1940. During *Barbarossa* many units were still equipped with the outdated 37mm gun-armed Panzer III. Limited production numbers also hampered the reorganization of the Panzertruppen started after Guderian took over from Lutz as Inspector and commander of XVI AK early in 1938. That same year two new Panzer divisions were formed, followed early in 1939 by the cadres of another one and the eventual reorganization of the Panzer units thanks to the limited availability of the new Panzer III and IV medium tanks. In August 1939 the tank establishment of a Panzer division now totalled some 310 tanks – a balanced unit when compared with the 'tank heavy' armoured formations of France and Britain. However, as Guderian experienced at first hand, there still was much to do. The first large-scale experience on the field during the seizure of Austria in March 1938 revealed two simple facts: having covered 700km (435 miles) in two days, the Panzer divisions were capable of the swift movements required to bring mobility back to the battlefield after the experience of World War I; also, having lost some 30 per cent of their tanks due to mechanical breakdowns, they were not yet ready for combat.

The solution to this problem was dramatically simple – tank repair and maintenance units were formed and attached to each Panzer division, and the Panzerwaffe developed a combat tactic that both tolerated a certain amount of losses due to breakdowns and combat and also developed a quick and efficient tank-recovery programme. It is not by chance that, in November 1938, Guderian's duties as an inspector changed from overseeing the recruiting, training, tactics and techniques of the Panzer units to the overseeing recruiting, training, tactics and techniques of most of the mechanized and motorized units of the army. The new Panzer division, the one consisting of a combination of tanks, infantry, artillery, reconnaissance, anti-tank units and services that made it capable of fighting and exploiting a favourable situation entirely on its own, was now a reality. And yet, as Nehring remarked, at the outbreak of war in September 1939 the 'schnelle Truppen' were entirely made of experimental units, still to be tested on the battlefield and largely in need of improvement.

A new form of warfare

Guderian raged when he was given command of XIX AK, temporarily renamed 'fortress staff Pomerania', at the mobilization of the German Army. What looked like a reserve corps was, in reality, one of the new motorized army corps raised for the planned attack against Poland (until 1942 both mechanized and motorized corps were simply named Armeekorps (motorisiert). With only one single Panzer division and two motorized infantry divisions, Guderian – who was deployed north, facing Danzig – had a limited range of objectives. Mostly, it was a case of his formation gaining useful experience on an actual battlefield. Even at this early stage, Guderian – whose past experience had been largely restricted to staff duties – displayed an aggressiveness unparalleled among other German generals of his background. Putting into practice the German concept of 'leading forward', which required commanders to move to the front to be able to assess the situation first-hand and react accordingly, he kept himself constantly on the move, showing up were spearheads were involved in heavy fighting, personally locating the 'centre of gravity' (*Schwerpunkt*) of the attack and motivating his men. Unlike other generals whose constant movement kept them out of touch with their staff, such as Rommel, Guderian made best use of modern communication systems by travelling in a radio-equipped command vehicle with which he kept himself in touch with corps command.

Plevno, Poland, 5 September 1939. Surrounded by a large group of officers and soldiers, Guderian describes the situation to Hitler. Between them is Oberst Rudolf Schmundt, Hitler's principal military adjutant. Behind Hitler, Heinrich Himmler can be seen. (IWM, HU 75351)

German soldiers conversing with men of the Red Army, September 1939, following the Polish campaign that saw them both fighting a mutual enemy. The Soviet contribution was essential to the early development of the Panzerwaffe, notably at the Soviet training field of Kazan (which the Germans renamed 'Kama'). (IWM, HU 5505)

Breakthrough at the Meuse, May 1940

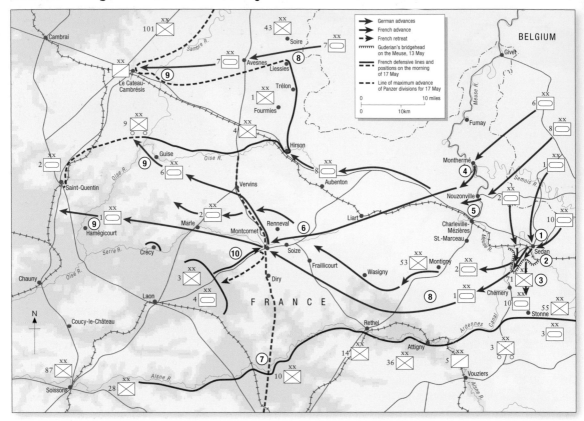

1. After the drive through the Ardennes, Guderian's XIX AK (mot.) reaches the Meuse at Sedan by the late evening of 12 May.

2. 13 May: the Meuse is crossed and a bridgehead is established across the river.

3. 14 May: the bridgehead is expanded in spite of French counterattacks from Chémery. Guderian detaches 10. Panzer-Division to cover the southern flank, while 2. and 1. Panzer-Divisionen advance west on the 15th.

4. After reaching the Meuse on 13 May, 6. Panzer-Division (part of Reinhardt's XXXXI AK (mot.)) establishes a bridgehead at Monthermé and starts advancing west early on the morning of the 15th.

5. 8. Panzer-Division, part of XXXXI AK (mot.), establishes a bridgehead on the Meuse during the night of 15 May.

6. 6. Panzer-Division's fast advance from the Meuse to Montcornet, which is reached in the late evening of 15 May after a drive of 55km (34 miles)

7. Line of maximum advance for the Panzer divisions established by Kleist in his order of 16 May (1630hrs), which reached Guderian at 0045hrs on the 17th.

8. Guderian's advance west to Montcornet, 15–16 May (bottom arrow). After establishing and securing a bridgehead on the Meuse at Dinant on 12–14 May, on the 15th Rommel's 7. Panzer-Division advances to the Franco-Belgian border and, during the night of 16 May, drives to Avesnes, which is reached at midnight (top arrow).

9. Ignoring Kleist's order, Guderian's forces continues their advance westwards of the 'halt line', which they had already crossed, and at 0700hrs on 17 May 1. Panzer-Division establishes a bridgehead on the Sambre river to the south of Saint-Quentin (bottom arrow). At the same time, XXXXI AK's 8. Panzer-Division establishes its own bridgehead on the Sambre to the north of Saint-Quentin on 17 May (centre arrow). Early in the morning of 17 May, Rommel's 7. Panzer-Division resumes its advance reaching the Sambre at 0600hrs and establishing a bridgehead at Le Cateau half an hour later (top arrow).

10. De Gaulle's 4e Division blindée counterattacks at Montcornet at noon on 17 May; after destroying a German column, its advance is halted by a mixed group of anti-tank and anti-aircraft guns of 1. Panzer-Division supported by a few tanks returning from repair shops, and by close air support.

Once again, Guderian experienced at first hand the full potential and limitations of the Panzer forces on the battlefield. On 9 September his corps, reinforced with the partly formed 10. Panzer-Division, started a deep penetration into Poland that ended at Brest-Litovsk. In ten days Guderian's XIX AK advanced about 330km (200 miles), at times against stiff resistance, losing only 4 per cent of its men, which amounted to more than 40 per cent of all the total losses amongst the Heeresgruppe Nord. Logistical problems inevitably occurred, such as when on 2 September XIX AK (mot.)'s vanguards ran out of fuel and the attack stalled. This was a major shortcoming, but the Panzer had also revealed itself as a decisive weapon, with only six to eight destroyed out of 350 employed. Following its successful baptism of fire the units were reorganized, with the four light divisions turned into Panzer divisions during the winter of 1939–40. Inside the Panzer divisions themselves, units were rearranged down to company and platoon level and doctrines were revised. It is certainly possible to discern the hand of Guderian in all of this.

The significance of the role played by Guderian in 1939–40 is revealed by his involvement in the planning for the attack on the West, Fall *Gelb*. In mid-November 1939 the staff of XIX AK (mot.) were moved west, first to Düsseldorf and then Coblenz, under Heeresgruppe A commanded by General Karl von Rundstedt, whose chief of staff was General Erich von Manstein – the eventual creator of the final plan of attack which envisaged a giant 'sickle cut' across the Ardennes to the Channel to cut off the bulk of enemy forces in Belgium and Holland. Although not directly involved in the development of the plan, Guderian was asked by Manstein for his opinion from the point of view of a Panzer commander. Having carefully checked the maps, and relying on his own knowledge of the terrain, Guderian reassured Manstein about the plan's feasibility. He stressed only one vital factor – that the greatest possible number of Panzer units be committed to the 'sickle' part of the plan, possibly all of them. Guderian would stress this factor again in a wargame held in Coblenz on 7 February 1940, from which it was ascertained that it would be possible to cross the Meuse at Sedan on the fifth day of the offensive, establish a bridgehead and from there advance west to Amiens. The plan was eventually drafted on 24 February 1940, and Guderian's XIX AK (mot.) was to play a key

A photo taken by Hermann Weper, an officer serving with Maschinengewehr-Bataillon 52, on 4 June 1940 following the seizure of Dunkirk. A 20mm Flak 38 gun, covered with a camouflage shelter quarter, is watching the shoreline, which is covered with debris left by the evacuating British forces. (IWM, COL 287)

A famous portrait of Guderian aboard his SdKfz 251/6 command vehicle in France, 1940. A former staff officer with very little combat experience, Guderian's energetic command and leadership qualities displayed during the campaigns in 1939–41 brought him often right to the very front. (The Tank Museum, 3052B1)

role in it. The whole concept was an evolution of theories dating back to the mid-1800s, first developed by Moltke the Elder, which focused on the concentration of forces, selection of a key point and use of speed to outmanoeuvre the enemy. This approach failed in 1914 with the Schlieffen Plan, but the motorization and mechanization of the German Army now made it much more possible. Guderian's motto 'Klotzen, nicht kleckern' ('boot them, don't spatter them', or 'strike concentrated not dispersed') was the simplest adaptation of Moltke's theories to modern warfare, while the development of the Panzer division as a combined arms formation, still led by the tank but supported by other units, was its basic instrument.

The bulk of the 'sickle' across the Ardennes was made of Paul Ewald von Kleist's Panzergruppe, which consisted of Guderian's XIX AK (mot.) – three Panzer divisions – General Hans-Georg Reinhardt's XXXXI AK (mot.) – two Panzer divisions and one motorized infantry division – and the XIV AK (mot.), with two divisions. All in all it included 134,000 men, 41,000 vehicles, 1,250 tanks and 362 reconnaissance vehicles; half of the total number of the Panzer divisions and about half the total German tank strength on the West. The first problem faced was one of traffic control. The reason the Ardennes was considered unsuitable for tanks was its highly wooded terrain and small roads, which were poorly marked and not suitable for heavy traffic. The solution was a carefully planned approach march to the targets, which saw Guderian's XIX AK (mot.) moving first followed then by Reinhardt's XXXXI AK (mot.) and finally by XIV AK (mot.). Obstacles, particularly rivers, had to be dealt with by the engineers who were tasked with clearing all the road obstacles and minefields before the Meuse and to support the crossing of the Meuse and Semois rivers, where pontoon bridges had to be built immediately after bridgeheads had been established. Clearly, any delay suffered by the spearhead units would have heavy repercussions on the follow-up ones and, potentially, might jam the whole operation since Reinhardt's troops were supposed to switch north after crossing the Belgian border to try and cross the Meuse to the north of Sedan, Guderian's XIX AK (mot.)'s objective.

Guderian and his staff's activity in preparation for this assault has been often overlooked, even though it was decisive for the eventual outcome. Junior commanders were to play a decisive role like never before and thus both Guderian and Nehring, his chief of staff, started a rigorous training programme intended to develop their own initiative while at the same time becoming experts in the leading of their own particular units. The programme was supervised by Guderian, who made continuous visits between February and May 1940 to the various training centres all around Germany. Infantry and engineers, in particular, trained in river crossing using assault rubber boats, while the latter trained to build pontoon bridges and to ferry vehicles using pontoon sections. Not that everything went according to plan; new batches of Panzer III and IV tanks were only delivered to Guderian's Panzer divisions on 12 March 1940, less than two months before the attack started. Feeling the pressure of time, commanders spared them and kept training tank crews with the old Panzer I and II models, much to Kleist's annoyance. It was only after he upbraided Guderian on this particular matter that the latter developed a special training programme to be completed in just ten days. In any case, Kleist ordered that company- and battalion-level exercises be held. The staff dealt with other matters as well. Checking the available maps, Nehring discovered that the army and Luftwaffe used different versions, which might have led to confusion. A solution was found in the development of a small-scale grid reference system which, along with appropriate markers on the field to distinguish friend from foe, enabled high level of accuracy when it came to air support.

This was another innovation in German tactics. As they only had half of the artillery deployed by Allied forces, the Germans relied on motorized artillery that could easily be redeployed or on air support from Stuka dive-bombers. The Luftwaffe also provided air defence, both through anti-aircraft artillery – which was also used against land targets – and fighter cover; the Luftwaffe also helped to remedy some of the logistical problems experienced in the Poland campaign. With every single Panzer Division consuming 226,000 litres of fuel every 100km (more when in combat), refuelling was clearly a problem in spite of the large availability of extra transport. A solution was found in the aerial resupply of forward units, a system developed at the very last moment with a series of exercises carried out on 8–10 April 1940 that provided the basis for what was a decisive innovation.

At 0535hrs on 10 May 1940 the German offensive in the West started, with Guderian's three Panzer divisions (1., 2. and 10.) crossing the border of Luxembourg on the Our River. The pace was quick, in spite of Belgian and French delaying actions, and by the following day the vanguards of 1. Panzer-Division had reached the Semois River, just before the Franco-Belgian border. Problems were caused by the chaotic traffic jams developing among the follow-up units and supplies moving behind the advanced columns of Guderian's XIX AK (mot.). Nevertheless, at 1815hrs on 12 May, well before Guderian had forecasted, the spearheads of 1. Panzer-Division approached the northern banks of the Meuse at Sedan. That same day Guderian, whose HQ in the Hotel

'Where to now?' Guderian seems to ask himself during the early days of the attack in the West in May 1940. In fact his knowledge of the Ardennes and of the terrain enabled him to plan a speedy advance for the three Panzer divisions of his XIX AK (mot.). (Private collection)

21

Hermann Weper's photo showing a group of German officers from the staff of Maschinengewehr-Bataillon 52 talking and resting just before entering Dunkirk on 4 June 1940. Even though Guderian criticized Hitler's decision to halt his troops shortly after the Channel had been reached, he later admitted that the area was unsuitable for mechanized units. (IWM, COL 292)

Fatal hours: Montcornet, 16 May 1940

On 13 May Guderian's XIX AK (mot.) had secured a bridgehead on the Meuse, which was expanded and secured during the following two days when follow-up troops reached the area. On the 16th, Guderian advanced west with both the 1. and 2. Panzer-Divisionen. The situation was confused and unclear, and a French counterattack was expected to deal with the 50km-wide (31-mile) breach of the front. On the same day, while Guderian's forces reached Montcornet which had already been seized by the 6. Panzer-Division, instructions arrived from General von Kleist ordering that the Panzer forces were not to advance west of Montcornet. Unaware of this order, Guderian had already ordered both Panzer divisions to advance west, which they did. This led to a clash on the 17th between Guderian and Kleist, with the former threatening to resign his command. The matter was eventually settled that same day, while Guderian's 1. Panzer-Division had already secured a bridgehead on the Oise river some 30km (19 miles) to the west of Montcornet.

In May 1940 Guderian **(1)** (who, during the campaign, was careful enough to wear a simple officers' coat, without the conspicuous red lapels of the general ones) travelled in an SdKfz 251/6 **(2)** armoured, half-tracked command vehicle along with his aide, Oberstleutnant Riebel **(3)** and a crew of tankers. Thanks to this, Guderian was able on 16 May to reach the HQ of 1. Panzer-Division at Omont, then the staff of 2. Panzer-Division at Poix-Terron and from there Montcornet. During the last stretch of this march, Guderian's command vehicle passed along the columns of marching infantry from 1. Panzer-Division. Fully confident of the success, they started to cheer their commander shouting phrases like 'Well done, old boy', and 'There's our old man', the 'lightning Heinz'. Once at Montcornet, Guderian quickly arranged with the commander of the 6. Panzer-Division the routes of advance for the three divisions and by the end of the following day they had already secured two bridgeheads on the Oise. Four days later, they had reached the Channel and closed the circle around the Allied armies.

Panorama in Buillon was bombed by the RAF, met with Kleist to observe the Luftwaffe's bombing of Sedan, carried out with absolute precision. In crossing the Meuse the Germans faced a number of serious problems, including a lack of adequate reconnaissance of the terrain and their inferiority in terms of firepower, given the fact that part of their artillery was still trapped in the busy roads of the Ardennes. However, in March a series of wargames had been held to study in detail the crossing of the Meuse at Sedan, which provided an impromptu, detailed and timely assault plan right in time for the crossing. This took place at 1600hrs on the 13th and, despite meeting fierce opposition from the French side, it managed to breach the defences and establish a large bridgehead about 5km (3 miles) wide and, at its southernmost wedge, 5km (3 miles) deep. What followed was the critical moment; on the morning of 14 May a French armoured counterattack was repulsed at Boulson; meanwhile, Schützen-Regiment 1 of the 1. Panzer-Division established a bridgehead on the Ardennes canal to the west. A prudent course of action would have been to regroup forces and secure the bridgehead against further counterattacks until the supporting infantry arrived and took over from the leading Panzer divisions. However, at 1400hrs on 14 May Guderian ordered both the 1. and 2. Panzer-Divisionen to move westwards, while the 10. Panzer-Division was left alone to defend the bridgehead at Sedan. This was not only a risk, but it was also contrary to Guderian's famous mantra of 'strike concentrated, not dispersed'. The French launched in fact a series of counterattacks against the 10. Panzer-Division which, supported by Infanterie-Regiment 'Grossdeutschland', was able to hold the front in spite of the overwhelming superiority of the French heavy tanks. Guderian's XIX AK (mot.) was not the only breakthrough on the Meuse, for on the 14–15th the river was crossed to the north by Reinhardt's XXXXI AK (mot.), as well as Hoth's XV AK (mot.) south of Dinant, but Guderian's position was decisive for the entire operation. By 15 May a breakthrough had been achieved with the 6. Panzer-Division at Montcornet and Rommel's 7. Panzer-Division 40km (25 miles) west of the Meuse. At 0045hrs on 17 May Guderian received an order issued by Kleist at 1630hrs on the 16th, stating that no advance west of Montcornet was to be made. This led to a major clash between Guderian and Kleist, with the former resigning from his command only to be ordered back to his post by a concerned Rundstedt. Eventually, Guderian was authorized to conduct a 'reconnaissance in force', which allowed his units some rest and refit before the ban on advance westwards was lifted on 19 May. That same day 2. Panzer-Division advanced 90km (55 miles) from its positions west of Saint-Quentin, reaching Abbeville, the final objective of the 'sickle cut', by 2030hrs. Eventually, by 0200hrs on the 20th, its vanguards reached the Channel at Noyelles.

This day marked the beginning of a new form of warfare, dominated by the well-established reality of motorization and mechanization. A reality owing much to the skills and capabilities of Heinz Guderian, who had proved in both his theories and their practical application on the battlefield how the world had changed. It did not mean, however, that the battle for France was over. A huge pocket containing some four enemy armies had been created, and the Germans still had to deal with it. On 21 May Guderian resumed the advance along the coast while a British counterattack was halted at Arras. The Panzer advance came to a standstill on the 24 May, when they stood at just 15km (9 miles) from Dunkirk, the last harbour in Allied hands. Hitler's 'halt order', eventually lifted on the 26th, is a perennial source of controversy which we do not have room to cover here. What is worth noting, however, is the situation of the Panzer forces with relation to the fact that, from Hitler's point of view, the war against France was far from over. The fact that the real invasion of the country (Fall *Rot*) was yet to start, meant that preserving the Panzer units was a necessity rather than just a luxury. And they did need to be preserved; when the halt order came, Guderian's corps had suffered some 50 per cent tank losses, and time was needed to recover and to restore the Panzer divisions' combat effectiveness. For this reason, two days after the advance was resumed, Guderian admitted that the chance had been lost and suggested that infantry dealt with the reduction of the Dunkirk pocket.

Guderian did not have much time to rest and reflect on the victory; on 1 June his corps was provisionally renamed Panzergruppe Guderian, with two motorized corps under his command. This elevated him to the same level as Kleist, whose newly reorganised Panzergruppe was to form the right wing of the German offensive against France, while Guderian's formed its left wing. Scheduled to attack five days after the attack on the right (western) wing had started on 5 June, Panzergruppe Guderian's objective was to reach the Swiss border – more than 300km (185 miles) to the south of the French defence line along the Somme–Aisne rivers – and surround the French 2e Groupe d'armées. In spite of the defeat suffered in May, the French Army was still quite strong and willing to defend its homeland. Kleist and Hoth's attacks on the Somme of 5 June initially met with stiff resistance, and it was only on 8–9 June that a wedge was driven into the French defences north of Paris. Not everywhere, though, with XVI AK (mot.) being halted north of Paris; it was pulled back and re-routed to the right wing of Guderian's Panzergruppe, whose attack was launched on 9 June with bridgeheads established over the Aisne by the following day. The pace of the advance was steady until 14 June, when the German army entered Paris and Guderian's forces reached Saint-Dizier. In the following days it turned into a real race with the vanguard of the Panzergruppe reaching the Swiss border on 17 June. With this the trap around the remnants of three French armies was closed, and another 500,000 French prisoners of war fell into Guderian's hands.

A motorized column of the SS-Panzergrenadier Division 'Das Reich', part of Guderian's Panzergruppe 2, during the opening stages of *Barbarossa*. (Carlo Pecchi)

Fall *Rot*, June 1940

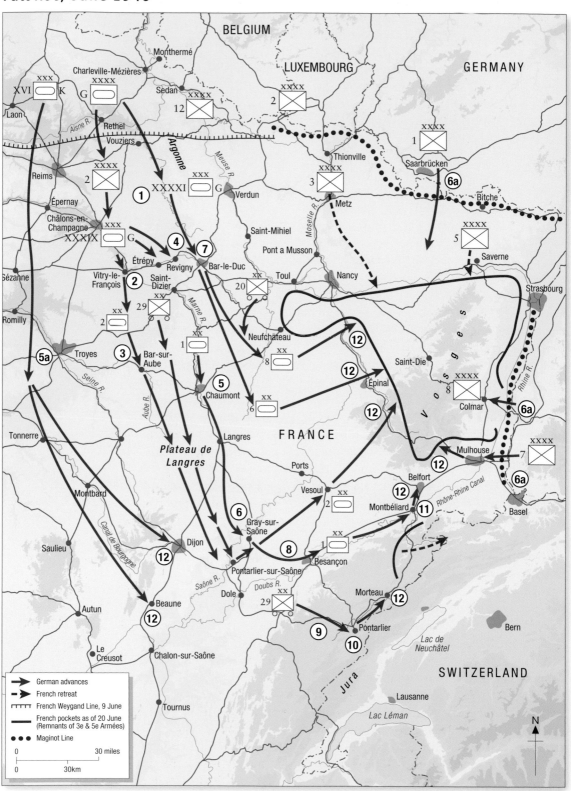

Legend:
- German advances
- French retreat
- French Weygand Line, 9 June
- French pockets as of 20 June (Remnants of 3e & 5e Armées)
- Maginot Line

0 — 30 miles
0 — 30km

N

1. After AOK 12's attack across the Aisne on 9 June, on 10–11 June XXXIX and XXXXI AK (mot.) (both part of the newly formed Panzergruppe Guderian) start their attack southwards, facing at first tough French resistance.
2. 2. Panzer-Division reaches Vitry-le-François on 13 June, crossing the Marne River on the following day.
3. On 15 June 2. Panzer-Division (XXXIX AK (mot.)) seizes Bar-sur-Aube.
4. On 13 June 1. Panzer-Division (XXXIX AK (mot.)) establishes a bridgehead on the Rhine–Marne canal at Étrépy.
5. 1. Panzer-Division reaches Chaumont on 14 June.
5a. XVI AK (mot.) (part of Panzergruppe Kleist) advances to the Seine, which is reached in the area of Troyes by 14 June.
6. On 15 June, after a drive across Langres, 1. Panzer-Division reaches Gray-sur-Saône.
6a. German attacks on the Maginot Line: 14 June (AOK 1, Operation *Tiger*) and 15 June (AOK 7, Operation *Kleiner Bär*).
7. XXXXI AK reaches Bar-le-Duc on 15 June.
8. On 16 June 1. Panzer-Division, having seized an intact bridge over the Saône, advances southwards seizing Besançon;

2. Panzer Division crosses the Saône at Pontarlier-sur-Saône and swings eastwards.
9. 29. Infanterie-Division (mot.) (XXXIX AK (mot.)) crosses the Saône on 16 June and moves south.
10. 29. Infanterie-Division (mot.) reaches Pontarlier on the Swiss border.
11. 1. Panzer-Division advances to Belfort, which is seized on 18 June.
12. The final advance of Panzergruppe Guderian: after reaching the Saône, 8. and 6. Panzer-Divisionen (XXXXI AK (mot.)) swing eastwards to the Moselle, where bridgeheads are established on 18 June. The 2. Panzer Division advances to the Moselle as well, establishing a bridgehead on 18–19 June, while on the 19th the 1. Panzer-Division makes contact with AOK 7. In the Vosges area the remnants of three French armies are surrounded. 29. Infanterie-Division (mot.) advances along the Swiss border, compelling the French XXXXV Corps to seek refuge across the Swiss border. Panzergruppe Kleist's XVI AK (mot.) advances to Dijon and the Saône.

The Eastern Front

The German victory in the West in 1940 was the result of an evolution in tactics and the technical improvements of an already sound and well-established doctrine dating back to the times of Moltke. It would not have been possible without the creation of the Panzerwaffe and, above all, its evolution in the two decisive years before 1940. There are few doubts that Heinz Guderian was not the man behind the first step, though he certainly played a decisive role in the second stage between 1938 and 1940. His theories proved correct, and his organizational work made the Panzer divisions a decisive instrument of warfare. Guderian also proved himself to be a skilled and capable field commander, who could train and inspire his men as well as lead them into battle with confidence. That does not mean there were no problems at all. The speed that was essential in order to surprise the enemy and thwart his defences also meant logistical troubles, heavy losses among the tanks and motor vehicles and the unsolved problem of follow-up infantry, who still marched at a pace that would have been familiar to the veterans of 1914–18. The case of the Dunkirk pocket is revealing: it took about two weeks to reduce the pocket after the ring had been closed in ten days, and a large number of men trapped inside it were able to escape. Back then, this was not a major problem since these men were not back on the battlefield, and the bulk of the enemy forces had been destroyed as an effective fighting force before the last stage of the campaign was started. The same problem was encountered in the early stages of Operation *Barbarossa*, the German attack on the Soviet Union that was conceived as a blitzkrieg effort to destroy the bulk of the Red Army that was stationed close to the German border. Time and space would play a decisive role in this campaign. Once again, the German Army was made up of a relatively small number of armoured and motorized divisions with the majority consisting of infantry divisions. Poorer roads slowed their advance down, as did the many pockets of Soviet troops left behind by the fast-advancing Panzer and motorized units. These were, in turn, to face the problem of the vast expanse of Russia. The distance covered by Guderian's forces in May 1940 to the Channel, some 300km (185 miles), was the same as that between their starting positions in June 1941 and their first objective, Minsk. The final objective of the first stage of the campaign, Smolensk, stood at about 700km (435 miles). This meant greater logistical problems, as well as unforeseen levels of attrition.

The objective of Guderian's Panzergruppe 2, which along with Hoth's Panzergruppe 3 was part of Heeresgruppe Mitte, was to advance into the Bialystok salient along parallel lines and to link up east of Minsk, thus trapping the bulk of the Red Army's forces deployed along the border area into a first major pocket. The second phase was an advance towards the Vitebsk–Smolensk–Yelnia–Roslavl area to establish bridgeheads across the Dnepr and in the upper Dvina, in order to prevent the Soviets from using these rivers as a defensive barrier. After this first stage there was some uncertainty as to what to do next; the general scheme was, at the beginning, to continue with the advance towards Moscow, but in July 1941 Hitler already wanted to have both *Panzergruppen* moved north, towards Leningrad, and south, towards the Donets basin. From Guderian's point of view, the plan started to go wrong long before the actual campaign. Forecasting heavy

A column from a Panzer division of Panzergruppe 2 on the move during *Barbarossa*. The poor Soviet road network and the large distances called for impromptu solutions, like carrying infantrymen on tanks, shown here on this Panzer II. (Carlo Pecchi)

resistance from the Red Army's units along the well-fortified border, the plan put infantry units to the fore with the aim of breaking through the Soviet defences and opening the way for the Panzer forces. Guderian did not like this approach as he thought, on the basis of his experience in the Ardennes, that having the infantry to the front would only slow his forces down by bogging them down in an overloaded and poor quality road network. Other problems arose soon after the campaign had started on 22 June 1941. Following a spectacular offensive, Hoth's and Guderian's forces linked up east of Minsk on 28 June, closing a grand total of some 300,000 Red Army soldiers into two different pockets (Bialystok and Minsk). The slow-moving infantry had only been able to complete the encirclement around the first pocket, leaving motorized and armoured forces to hold the ring around the second. In order to free HQs for the advance west, an army command held in reserve was activated to take control of the Bialystok pocket and on 26 June Kluge's AOK 4 took control over both *Panzergruppen* provoking a furious reaction from Guderian.

Guderian first clashed with Günther von Kluge in September 1939, when part of his XIX AK (mot.) fell under control of the latter's AOK 4. This was the beginning of a long-lasting antagonism that only came to an end in July 1944. On 2 and 4 July, there were some 'communication' problems between AOK 4 and units of Panzergruppe 2, which enabled the latter to continue their advance east neglecting the Minsk pocket. Kluge had Guderian summoned to his HQ and threatened a court martial, but Guderian 'put his mind at rest on that score'. In fact, Guderian had the tacit approval of both the army staff and of the army group command to continue with his advance towards Smolensk, and the best Kluge could do was to exercise some restraint on his impetuous advance.

There were no solutions to the problems the Germans were experiencing at this early stage of the campaign. A lack of forces prevented them from sealing the pockets and reducing them efficiently, with the consequence that large groups of units were either trying to move eastwards or threatening the rear areas of the most advanced units. New problems such as the inadequate road network that, under the strain of hundreds of vehicles, turned into quagmires at the first rain, combined old ones, like the lack of spare parts and repair facilities that prevented damaged tanks from becoming operational again. By 7 July, Panzergruppe 2 had lost 10 per cent of its tanks, and two of its Panzer Divisions were down to some 35 per cent operational. Losses and the stiffening Soviet resistance slowed down the pace of advance and it was not until 10 July that Panzergruppe 2 crossed the Dnepr bearing in mind Guderian's order: 'All the commanders of the Panzergruppe and their troops must disregard threats to the flanks and the rear. My divisions know only to press forward.' This led to another clash between Kluge and Guderian, who won the argument and pressed forwards without waiting for the follow-up infantry who were still moving out from the Minsk pocket, officially reduced on the 8th.

The crossing of the Dnepr took place without too many problems, and by 13 July two other pockets of Soviet troops were trapped at Orscha and Mogilev; by the evening of 15 July the spearheads of 29. Infanterie-Division (mot.) reached the outskirts of Smolensk, which was taken the following day. Things were not going smoothly, however, since a Red Army counterattack against Guderian's left flank started on 13 July and caused great concern. Once again the forces at Guderian's disposal were not enough to accomplish all the tasks and the pocket around Smolensk

A light SdKfz 222 armoured car of Kleist's Panzergruppe 1 in Russia, 1941. Along with Guderian's Panzergruppe 2 it was responsible for the Kiev pocket which, even though it was a diversion from the main German advance on Moscow, destroyed a large number of Soviet troops. (Carlo Pecchi)

Guderian congratulates Leutnant Hohnstetter, a tank commander of Panzer-Regiment 35, 4. Panzer-Division, which captured Orel on 3 October 1941 during the early stages of Operation *Typhoon*, the advance to Moscow. (The Tank Museum, 3222A5)

was not closed because his forces were too weak to link up with Hoth's, while his decision to send a Panzer division east towards Yelnya, with the aim of opening the road to Moscow, further aggravated the situation. Thus, while the southern flank was secured and some progress was made north of Smolensk, between 17 and 20 July the battle focused on the Yelnya salient, while Guderian waited for the infantry to catch up. This turned out to be one of the biggest mistakes made by Guderian during Operation *Barbarossa*. Supply problems, along with the Soviet decision to mount a strong counteroffensive in the Smolensk area, turned the battle for the Yelnya salient into one of attrition that hardly suited the German blitzkrieg strategy. On 19 July Guderian eventually issued an order to the *Panzergruppe* clearly stating that, having secured the area south-east of Smolensk, there would be a rest and refit period. The order was cancelled the following day and the battle continued. By 26 July the pocket around Smolensk was closed when spearheading units of Panzergruppen 2 and 3 linked east of the city, even though they were too weak to face the Soviet counterattacks and prevent portions of the three surrounded Soviet armies to escape the trap along a narrow corridor by 4 August. On 31 July Guderian also unleashed the troops on his right flank and, with a hook movement, seized Roslavl and surrounded a large group of enemy units.

The decision taken by Hitler to send Guderian's forces to the south, with the aim of surrounding the Soviet forces at Kiev rather than to continue with their advance toward Moscow, is perhaps as debated now as it was back then. Guderian himself did not agree with it and flew to Hitler's HQ on 23 August

Operation *Barbarossa*, June–July 1941

A common sight during the early stages of Operation *Barbarossa*: a Panzer III tank moving over an unpaved road past a Russian village, passing along a destroyed Soviet T-34 tank while a Horch staff car from the Panzer regiment's HQ is parked on the other side of the road. The T-34 (like the heavy KV-1) tank came as a surprise to the Germans, who lacked an adequate anti-tank weapon to deal with it. The Panzer III, the standard German main battle tank in 1941, even when armed with a 50mm gun (others were armed with a 37mm gun), was helpless against it. In November 1941 a Panzer III belonging to 3. Panzer-Division of Panzergruppe 2 fired several rounds at 50m and even 20m against a T-34 without achieving any effect.

to try and convince him to change his mind, a task in which he failed. Here, too, opinions diverge, since some claim that Guderian gave up with his attempt, while others assume he had no chance of success in any case. Both positions are probably true as Guderian was just one of many top-level generals who failed to get Hitler to change his mind, while he also did not press his case to the point of resignation as he had done in the past; whether this was because he did not want to jeopardize his position on a matter of principle or, as some have assumed, because he had been 'bought' with the Eichenlaub to his Ritterkreuz and the promise of reinforcements, we shall very likely never know. As early as 24 August, back in his HQ, Guderian began to prepare the new offensive by switching two of his corps to the south to seize decent jump-off positions. The offensive started on 5 September and ended ten days later when his forces linked up with Kleist's Panzergruppe 1 at Lokhvitsa, closing the largest pocket ever made in the war. By then Hitler had ordered a resumption in the advance towards Moscow, a much harder task now than before. Not because the Red Army had taken advantage of the Kiev diversion to prepare its defences west of Moscow, but because the German forces were simply too worn out to push as hard as they had done so far. Strain and supply problems had taken their toll, and by September 1941 some 1,700 tanks out of the 3,400 deployed in June 1941 had been lost (only 137 replacements tanks had been sent). By 5 September only 47 per cent of the tanks on the Eastern Front were operational, with the Panzer Divisions being down to an average 34 per cent. Guderian's Panzergruppe 2 was in worse shape than the three others, having only 21 per cent of its tanks operational. And yet, on 30 September it was on the move again, this time heading for Moscow.

Guderian's new drive towards Moscow started with a breakthrough of the Soviet positions and another swift advance, leading his Panzergruppe 2 to seize Orel on 3 October and to close another pocket, the one around Bryansk

During Operation *Typhoon* the German Army faced the grim conditions of a Russian winter for the first time. This had a desperate effect not only on motor vehicles and tanks, but also on the men, who had not been equipped with appropriate clothing and equipment. (Carlo Pecchi)

Smolensk, July–August 1941

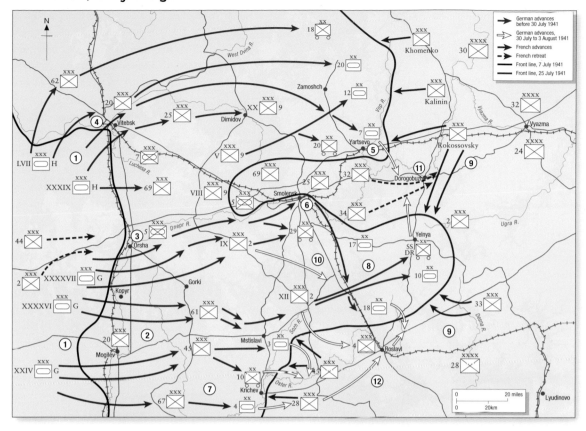

1. Guderian needs to decide whether to halt the advance and wait for the infantry units to catch up with the Panzers, or to continue the advance while remnants of the Red Army units encircled in the Minsk pocket are still trying to escape eastwards.

2. XXIV and XXXXVI Panzer Korps cross the Dnepr river on 10–11 July to the north and south of Mogilev, surrounding the 20th Soviet Army. By 16 July the 10. Panzer-Division, leading XXXXVI Panzer Korps' advance, reaches the Smolensk–Roslavl road.

3. XXXXVII Panzer Korps of Guderian's Panzergruppe 2 crosses the Dnepr on 10–11 July, enveloping Orsha from the south and advancing towards Smolensk south of the Dnepr bend.

4. On 6–7 July, Hoth's Panzergruppe 3 crosses the Dvina north of Vitebsk with LVII and XXXIX Panzer Korps; the battle for Vitebsk lasts two days between 8 and 9 July, when it falls into German hands

5. In spite of heavy Soviet counterattacks, Hoth's Panzergruppe 3 advances eastwards and, by 15 July, the 7. Panzer-Division reaches Yartsevo; the 20. Panzer-Division establishes a bridgehead across the Vop River and the northern pincer of the Smolensk pocket is formed.

6. On 16 July, 29. Infanterie-Division (mot.) seizes most of Smolensk while 17. Panzer-Division (both from XXXXVII Panzer Korps) advances further east along the Dnepr. This is the southern pincer of the Smolensk pocket, which is, however, far from being sealed.

7. While still dealing with the Mogilev pocket, XXIV Panzer Korps advances east, facing heavy counterattacks from Timoshenko's

Western Front, eventually a line along the Sozh–Oster river is established.

8. With a dash forward started on 17 July, 10. Panzer-Division reaches Yelnya and seizes it on 19–20 July, only to face strong Soviet counterattacks.

9. On 20 July, Zhukov orders a major counteroffensive using new reinforcements, grouped into 'operational groups' named after their commanders; these start to counterattack the German positions at Yartsevo and Yelnya the following day, while to the south counterattacks are also launched against the German positions on the Sozh River.

10. Between 20 and 26 July, both Panzergruppen 2 and 3 are at a standstill and having to deal with both Soviet counterattacks and the need to reorganize. This includes the redeployment to the south of 18. Panzer-Division and, later, 29. Infanterie-Division (mot.).

11. 26 July, the pincer around Smolensk eventually closes with the link up between 20. Infanterie-Division (mot.) and 7. Panzer-Division east of the city, even though elements of the encircled Soviet 16th, 19th and 20th armies manage to break through to the east by 4 August.

12. On 31 July, before completing its redeployment, Panzergruppe 2 starts its attack south with XXIV Panzer Korps attacking on both sides of the Oster River followed by XXXXVII Panzer Korps on 1 August; that same day the 4. Panzer-Division seizes Roslavl eventually surrounding and destroying most of Soviet 28th Army's 'Group Kachalov'.

During Operation *Typhoon* in the winter of 1941 weather conditions, along with the poor road network, often restricted movement to fully tracked vehicles only. The contrast between the white camouflaged tank and the infantry, still wearing the grey-green overcoat, is striking. (Carlo Pecchi)

with three Soviet armies inside, by the 8th. The first Soviet line of defence before Moscow had been broken. The pace of advance slowed down in mid to late October for several reasons – reinforcements and supplies were brought forward, the weather turned roads into quagmires, and part of Guderian's forces were tied up in the clearing of pockets. Having secured some supplies, and thanks to a Soviet mistake, Guderian was the first to resume the advance on 22 October, firstly with an unsuccessful attack at Mtsensk, then with a successful drive across the Soviet defences to the north of it, at Bolkhov the following day. By 28 October Kampfgruppe Eberbach of 4. Panzer-Division broke through the Soviet defences south of Tula, which it tried to seize with a *coup de main* on the 29th, albeit unsuccessfully. Once more the advance was halted by a number of factors and, while Guderian regrouped his forces in the Tula–Orel area, he also had to deal with a Soviet counterattack threatening his right flank. Only on 18 November was Guderian able to resume the offensive, but his schedule was overrun by a new Soviet counterattack that was repulsed with the use of motorized infantry divisions. Only as late as 24 November did Guderian's final assault against Tula start, with three Panzer divisions trying to envelop the town from the north-east. For a few days it looked like the long awaited breakthrough was close at hand, with the 17. Panzer-Division advancing north towards Venev and, 4. Panzer-Division's attempt to seize Tula on 2–4 December. But by 4–5 December the offensive had come to an halt, and Guderian started to regroup his units to favourable defensive positions. On 5–6 December the Soviet counteroffensive started, spreading panic amongst the Germans. On 7 December the Soviet attack in the Tula area threatened XXIV AK (mot.)'s positions, and Guderian eventually ordered his forces out of the Tula salient, withdrawing to shorter defensive positions some 80km (50 miles) to the west. Facing a serious threat to his forces, some of which had already been surrounded, Guderian started a major withdrawal to the Susha–Oka rivers in front of Orel, taking command of AOK 2 on 14 December (the new command was provisionally renamed Armeegruppe Guderian).

At this point, Guderian's command capabilities were being questioned. Hitler believed the German Army was not prepared to fight an elastic battle of defence (rightly, as it turned out) and on 17 December ordered him to stand fast. Three days later Guderian flew to Hitler's HQ and asked him personally for permission to withdraw, which the latter denied. Back in his own command, Guderian carried out the intended withdrawals, thus violating Hitler's direct orders. After one final clash with Kluge, Guderian asked to be relieved, which he was on 26 December 1941 along with 40 other generals.

Generalinspekteur der Panzertruppen

More than two years elapsed between Guderian's last field command and his new appointment, on 28 February 1943, as Generalinspekteur der Panzertruppen, during which the German Army suffered serious defeats at Stalingrad and El Alamein that, eventually, pushed it onto the defensive. When Guderian took over his new role, the Panzertruppen were at their lowest ebb. Five of the 27 Panzer divisions that had been formed up to late 1942 were disbanded between February and March 1943, followed by another four between May and September (three were being rebuilt in Germany). By early July 1943, when the attack against Kursk started, there only were 23 Panzer divisions in the inventory of the German Army (16 on the Eastern Front) plus 11 Panzergrenadier ones (previously motorized infantry divisions, now with a tank battalion), seven

Waffen-SS Panzer divisions, and the Panzergrenadier and Panzer divisions of the Luftwaffe. Not only that but most of the Panzer divisions deployed on the Eastern Front had only a single Panzer battalion, often still equipped with updated versions of the old Panzer III and IV. Guderian realized immediately that a major reorganization was needed. His short-term aim, by the end of 1943, was to create a fixed number of Panzer divisions that could be brought to a level of combat efficiency. In the long term, by spring 1944, he planned a restoration of the combat power of the German Panzer arm.

The first step was to obtain full control of the German armoured forces, a basic prerequisite given the chaotic organization that had developed in the previous year. In order to do this Guderian managed to persuade Hitler to subordinate the office of the Generalinspekteur der Panzertruppen directly to

A Panzer III from the HQ of a Panzer Abteilung has got bogged down while negotiating a stream in Russia and has halted the whole Panzer column, with a Panzer IV tank immediately behind. (Carlo Pecchi)

Until Guderian's appointment as Generalinspekteur der Panzertruppen, Germany's tank production was uncoordinated, which wasted both time and resources. Ninety samples of the Ferdinand or Elefant tank destroyer (first unsatisfactorily employed at Kursk) were built in spring 1943 following Hitler's order, principally as a way to compensate Porsche for having not chosen his prototype for the Tiger tank. (Nik Cornish, WH 833)

Moscow, November–December 1941

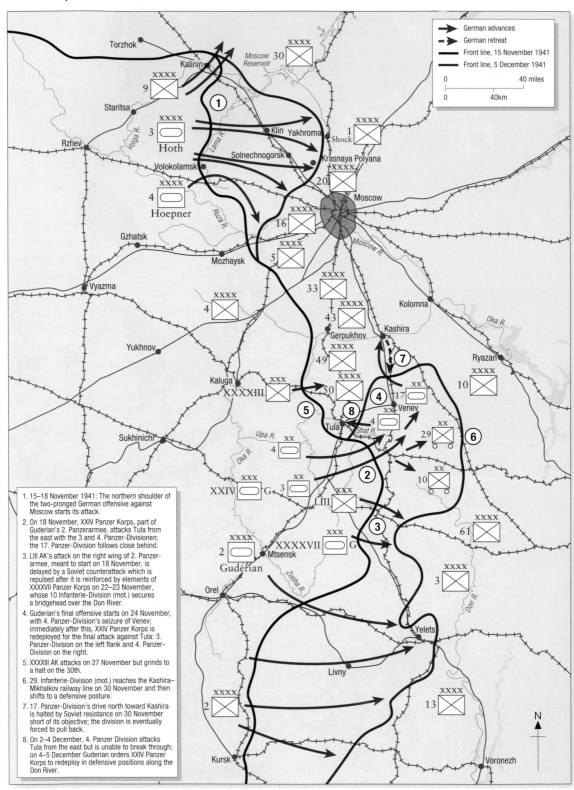

Legend:
- German advances
- German retreat
- Front line, 15 November 1941
- Front line, 5 December 1941

0 — 40 miles
0 — 40km

Torzhok
Kalinin
Moscow Reservoir
30 ✕✕✕✕
Staritsa
9 ✕✕✕✕
Rzhev
3 ✕✕✕✕ Hoth
Volga R.
Lama R.
Klin Yakhroma
1 ✕✕✕✕ Shock
Solnechnogorsk
Krasnaya Polyana
Volokolamsk
Ruza R.
20 ✕✕✕✕
4 ✕✕✕✕ Hoepner
Moscow
16 ✕✕✕✕
Gzhatsk
Mozhaysk
5 ✕✕✕✕
Moscow R.
Vyazma
4 ✕✕✕✕
33 ✕✕✕✕
Kolomna
43 ✕✕✕✕
Oka R.
Yukhnov
Gerpukhov
Kashira
49 ✕✕✕✕
7
Ryazan
10 ✕✕✕✕
Kaluga
XXXXIII ✕✕✕
50 ✕✕✕✕
17 ✕✕
4
Venev
5
8
4 ✕✕
Tula
Shat R.
29 ✕✕✕
6
Upa R.
4 ✕✕
Oka R.
2
10 ✕✕✕
Sukhinichi
XXIV ✕✕ G
3 ✕✕
LIII ✕✕✕
3
61 ✕✕✕✕
2 ✕✕
XXXXVII ✕✕✕ G
Mtsensk
Guderian
Zusha R.
3 ✕✕✕✕
Orel
Don R.
Yelets
Livny
2 ✕✕✕✕
13 ✕✕✕✕
Kursk
Voronezh

N

1. 15–18 November 1941: The northern shoulder of the two-pronged German offensive against Moscow starts its attack.

2. On 18 November, XXIV Panzer Korps, part of Guderian's 2. Panzerarmee, attacks Tula from the east with the 3 and 4. Panzer-Divisionen; the 17. Panzer-Division follows close behind.

3. LIII AK's attack on the right wing of 2. Panzer-armee, meant to start on 18 November, is delayed by a Soviet counterattack which is repulsed after it is reinforced by elements of XXXXVII Panzer Korps on 22–23 November, whose 10 Infanterie-Division (mot.) secures a bridgehead over the Don River.

4. Guderian's final offensive starts on 24 November, with 4. Panzer-Division's seizure of Venev; immediately after this, XXIV Panzer Korps is redeployed for the final attack against Tula: 3. Panzer-Division on the left flank and 4. Panzer-Division on the right.

5. XXXXIII AK attacks on 27 November but grinds to a halt on the 30th.

6. 29. Infanterie-Division (mot.) reaches the Kashira–Mikhalkov railway line on 30 November and then shifts to a defensive posture.

7. 17. Panzer-Division's drive north toward Kashira is halted by Soviet resistance on 30 November short of its objective; the division is eventually forced to pull back.

8. On 2–4 December, 4. Panzer Division attacks Tula from the east but is unable to break through; on 4–5 December Guderian orders XXIV Panzer Korps to redeploy in defensive positions along the Don River.

Hitler (who was commander-in-chief of the German Army), so that it was no longer subject to the whims of the army staff.

This gave Guderian strong, though not unlimited, control over the Panzertruppen – which included Panzer, Panzergrenadier and motorized infantry units, armoured reconnaissance and anti-tank troops, plus later the heavy assault gun (Sturmgeschütz) units; these all formed part of the Panzer

and the Panzergrenadier divisions. Guderian was directly responsible for the organization and training of the independent armoured units and the Panzer and Panzergrenadier divisions of the army, a task he was to carry out in cooperation with the chief of army staff, and he also had the right to issue general directives on the matter of organization and training to the armoured and mechanized units of the Waffen-SS and the Luftwaffe. His specific requests concerning the development of weapons and their production were also routed through Hitler in close cooperation with the Minister for Weapons and Ammunitions, Albert Speer. Guderian also had complete control over the home army part of the Panzertruppen – the replacement and training units (one of his duties was to ensure a constant flow of replacements, both personnel and vehicles, to front-line units), plus all the schools. He was also responsible for the collection of combat experiences and the drafting of new technical and tactical guidelines, which in turn gave Guderian the right to inspect every armoured and motorized unit.

With these powers in place Guderian began the major work of reorganization. His declared aim was the creation of 'tank heavy' Panzer divisions based around two Panzer regiments (some 400 tanks), though the actual tables of organization published had only a single regiment, with some 200. Guderian also planned to concentrate all new tank units – Tiger, Panther and 'a proportion of' Sturmgeschütz units – in the Panzer divisions and corps, and then only in the decisive theatres – the secondary ones had to make do with captured vehicles – under experienced commanders who knew how to

Though outdated, the Panzer III was still in widespread use throughout 1943, and the tank carried on in production till August of that year. This is a typical mixed unit on the Eastern Front equipped with both the Panzer III (one of them with a flamethrower) and the Panzer IV. (Nik Cornish, WH 821)

The 47mm gun Panzerjäger I was the first of its type, and a clear attempt to turn the old, machine-gun-equipped Panzer I into a real AFV. The white 'G', for 'Panzergruppe Guderian', was first used in June 1940 in France and then again in 1941. (Nik Cornish, WH 911)

use them properly. In this way he hoped to restore the combat efficiency of the Panzertruppen to something approaching its blitzkrieg-era peak. The timescale for this was one year, so that by spring 1944 Guderian hoped that his rebuilt Panzer arm would be able defeat the enemy on the battlefield once more.

A critical factor in this was the manner in which the Panzer

A column of late-model Panzer IV Ausf. G tanks crossing a Russian river over an improvised bridge, 1943–44. Although it was not the best tank in the German inventory, the production of the Panzer IV was continued on Guderian's advice in order to provide a suitable main battle tank until the Panther became available in large quantities. (Private collection)

regiments were to be reequipped in order to restore their full combat effectiveness, while at the same time those on the front line were still kept up to strength. By early 1943 German tank production was at a critical point. Most of the old types of tanks, including the Panzer III, were no longer suitable for the front given their lack of armour protection and weak armament. The Panzer IV was being upgraded and was still a viable tank, while the Tiger was only considered suitable as a support weapon, as its weight and lack of manoeuvrability made it less than ideal in an offensive role. The new Panzer V Panther tank, which had good armour protection and a high-velocity gun, was the new main battle tank intended to regain combat superiority in the battlefield. The problem was, however, that the Panther was still in the initial stages of its production and was both lacking in numbers and suffering from serious reliability issues.

Guderian's reorganization plan, outlined in a memorandum dated 13 May 1943, called for three of the 16 Panzer divisions deployed on the Eastern Front to be pulled out to rest and refit, and one Panzer battalion to be brought up

A fully armoured motorized infantry unit parading in France. Guderian was a strong advocate of the use of APCs, and only after his appointment as Generalinspekteur der Panzertruppen was their production dramatically increased with most Panzer divisions having one Panzergrenadier battalion equipped with them. (Carlo Pecchi)

to strength and fully equipped with Panzer IVs, while at least 15 Panzer divisions were to have the other battalion equipped with the new Panthers. This figure was a result of estimated production numbers, with a grand total of 1,700 Panther tanks being produced between May and December 1943. Excluding 230 Panthers reserved for the training units, all others were destined for front-line units even though, according to Guderian's own estimate, full combat readiness could not be reached before spring 1944 given the time necessary to train the battalions. The

downside to this plan was that the Panzer divisions still fighting on the Eastern Front were to be left with one single Panzer battalion for about a year, with all the operational difficulties that implied. Guderian's solution was to use the new Sturmgeschütz vehicles to create provisional Panzer battalions, though, given their limitations, they were only to be used in support of Panzer or Panzergrenadier units. This solution faced strong opposition from within the army as the Sturmgeschütz was intended to provide armoured support to the infantry divisions. The first 11 Sturmgeschütz battalions were deployed in 1941,

German infantry inspecting a T-34 tank during the early stages of *Barbarossa*. The tank was invulnerable to every gun except the 88mm and came as a big shock to the Germans who considered it could have been a 'war-winning weapon', had it not been for the poor use the Soviets made of it. (Nik Cornish, WH 165)

A Waffen-SS crew manning a 75mm Pak 40 in the winter of 1944–45. Anti-tank guns became more and more important in the last years of the war given the lack of AFVs. (Carlo Pecchi)

increasing in number to 30 by summer 1943 (mostly on the Eastern Front), but their effectiveness was always limited, and losses increased dramatically from mid-1943 as a clear consequence of insufficient training. As a result only a limited number of Panzer divisions on the Eastern Front had a second Sturmgeschütz-equipped Panzer battalion, while the overall German ability to counter Soviet armour stayed at about the same level.

A production line of early Tiger I tanks. Although it had an excellent gun and heavy armour, the Tiger was a very expensive tank to build (each one cost 250,000 Marks without guns and equipment) and its fuel consumption was very high, giving it an operational radius of only 60km in rough terrain from its 530-litre tanks. (Carlo Pecchi)

On 1 June 1944 there was a grand total of 31 Panzer divisions, plus 16 Panzergrenadier divisions. The only change was that a single army Panzer division had been created from training units (the Panzer Lehr), while five Waffen-SS divisions had been upgraded from Panzergrenadier divisions and the Luftwaffe's 'Hermann Göring' Division had been formed as well. Also, not all the Panzer divisions had the intended Panther-equipped battalion. Although production figures had matched Guderian's estimates (1,848 in 1943, another 1,468 by May 1944), the actual number of Panther-equipped battalions was not reached by June 1944. Moreover, some were not preserved as a strategic reserve but were rather used here and there to face occasional threats like the Allied landing at Anzio, Italy – what Guderian considered as a secondary theatre. All in all, only 14 Panther battalions were operational by June 1944 – nine with army divisions (four Panzer plus one Panzergrenadier Division on the Eastern Front, three in the West), and the other five with the Waffen-SS Panzer divisions (one on the Eastern Front, the others in the West).

The tank battle at Kursk, July 1943

Guderian was appointed Generalinspekteur der Panzertruppen on 28 February 1943, four months before the offensive against Kursk was launched on 5 July. Guderian, a staunch opponent of Operation *Zitadelle*, spent most of these months supervising the development of the new Panther tank. Intended to be the new German main battle tank, the one that should have restored battle superiority, it suffered heavily from teething problems and was far from ready for the front in July 1943. Two hundred of the 800 Panthers built by 1 July were deployed at Kursk with Panzer-Regiment 39 (Panther Regiment von Lauchert). Though only 42 were lost to enemy action by 16 July when the offensive ended, the regiment was left with only 43 operational tanks because all the others had suffered breakdowns or battle damage.

Chef des Stabes des Oberkommando des Heeres

Above: Infantry marching past a column of Sturmgeschütz IIIs. This assault gun was intended to provide the infantry with armoured gun support but, from 1943, it was also widely used in an anti-tank role. (Carlo Pecchi)

Below: A Panzer II tank moves alongside a Tiger I at Anzio, Italy, early in 1944. Although against Guderian's instructions to concentrate all the modern tanks in the main battle fronts in the east and the west, Tiger and Panther units also served in Italy. (Carlo Pecchi)

Guderian's initial organizational changes as Generalinspekteur der Panzertruppen were not as successful as he had hoped, as a remark by the commander of Panzergruppe West emphasizes: in spite of improved weapons and vehicles, the 1944 divisions only possessed one-third of the combat strength of a 1939 Panzer division. Guderian retained his position as Generalinspekteur even after his appointment as Chef des Stabes des OKH following the failed plot to assassinate Hitler on 20 July 1944. He was therefore not in much of a position to appreciate the improvement in the situation of the Panzertruppen in the autumn–winter of 1944 as he was occupied with other matters.

In the face of the continual Red Army offensives there was little Guderian could actually do given the lack of both troops and weapons, not to mention the constant interference from Hitler. The relationship between the two was troublesome, and Guderian clashed several times with him. However, he loyally carried out his orders and appears to have been, at least to some extent, a supporter of the 'hold every inch of ground' strategy. This could have arisen from his experiences outside Moscow in December 1941, or from the fact that Guderian's homeland was in eastern Germany and in immediate danger of attack. In August 1944, with Heeresgruppe Nord in danger of being cut off by the northern prong of the Soviet summer offensive, Guderian only organized a weak counterattack by Heeresgruppe Mitte and, when this failed and the army group wanted to pull back, he could only reply that, though he did not

agree with this, Hitler would not allow the retreat on political grounds. In the end, Heeresgruppe Nord was trapped in a small pocket in the Courland. On 8 August, Guderian was informed by HQ Heeresgruppe Südukraine that they needed to consider a strategic withdrawal to the Carpathian mountains and the lower Danube in case the Romanians became unreliable. Having consulted with Hitler, Guderian replied that he 'hoped' to be able to give such an order in time. A few days after the Soviet attack started on 20 August the Romanians became very unreliable and refused to carry on fighting. Very soon the German forces – those able to – started a hasty withdrawal to a line on the Carpathians–lower Danube. Romania surrendered a few days later, switching sides and joining the Soviet Union. Bulgaria followed suit and, in early September, it was the turn of Hungary to shift towards the Soviets. Guderian reacted swiftly by sending Panzer units to rest and refit close to Budapest. The Hungarian leader Admiral Horthy was arrested and replaced with the loyal leader of the Arrow-Cross party Szalasi. Guderian declared the 'political battle' won and called for Hungarians and Germans to defend the front.

This was his only victory on the Eastern Front. In mid-December 1944, facing the threat of a Soviet encirclement of Budapest, Guderian repeatedly urged the commander of Heeresgruppe Süd to start an armoured counteroffensive against the Red Army's northern prong. However, this counteroffensive became bogged down with meagre results because of a lack of infantry support for the Panzer spearheads. Guderian's only reaction was to order that every single unit, from divisions to single platoons, was to attack the enemy. By the end of the month, when the ring was about to close, Guderian, who had to this point refused proposals for an evacuation of the city, changed his mind and decided again to place the decisions into Hitler's hands. Needless to say his order was simple: Budapest was to be held until relieved by an offensive. This was at the same time as the German offensive in the Ardennes, which Guderian had opposed vehemently as it diverted valuable forces from the defence of the Eastern Front. A visit by Guderian to HQ Heeresgruppe Süd on 5 January 1945 confirmed how serious the situation was. Once again Hitler refused to countenance any kind of withdrawal, and when the

Above: A mid-production Tiger I being repaired on the Eastern Front, 1944. The overall dispersion of the Tiger and other AFVs in independent units in the final years of the war caused many problems in terms of maintenance and recovery. (Carlo Pecchi)

Below: An early Panther production line. Developed in response to the T-34, its production started in September 1942 but was plagued by several problems, and instead of the 250 tanks requested for May 1943, only 196 could be deployed at Kursk on 5 July. (Carlo Pecchi)

The Eastern Front, June 1944–April 1945

Legend:
- Soviet advances, 22 June 1944
- Soviet advances, 13 July 1944
- Soviet advances, August 1944
- Soviet advances, 20 August 1944
- Soviet advances, 14 September 1944
- Soviet advances, 24 September 1944
- Soviet advances, 12 January 1945
- Front line, June 1944
- Front line, September 1944
- Front line, mid-December 1944
- Front line, March 1945
- German borders, 1939
- Polish, Lithuanian, Latvian, Estonian and Soviet Union borders, 1939
- Polish territory annexed by Germany, 1939
- German and Soviet Union border, 1940–41
- Romanian border, 1940
- National borders, late 1941

1. The Soviet summer offensive (Operation *Bagration*) starts on 22 June 1944; by the end of July it has destroyed most of the German Heeresgruppe Mitte, whose remnants are pushed back to the 1939 Polish border.
2. The Soviet 1st Ukrainian Front attacks in southern Poland from 13 July 1944 and pushes the German Heeresgruppe Nord Ukraine beyond the Vistula by the end of August.
3. The Soviet summer offensive, launched in August 1944, pushes the German Heeresgruppen Nord and Mitte back to East Prussia, Warsaw and, to the north, close to the Baltic.
4. The 2nd and 3rd Ukrainian Fronts attack in the Balkans from 20 August 1944; by 25 August Romania has surrendered and switched sides, joining the Soviet Union (Bulgaria surrenders on 9 September 1944) and bringing most of the territory under Soviet control. By 29 August the Red Army is at the Danube. (Note: Finland surrendered to the Soviet Union on 4 September 1944.)
5. A new offensive is launched on 14 September 1944 against the German Heeresgruppe Nord; by late September to mid-October this leads to the clearing of the Baltic states leaving only German pockets in the Courland peninsula and at Memel (held by Heeresgruppe Courland).
6. On 24 September the Red Army starts its offensive against Hungary and Yugoslavia; by mid-December most of Hungary is occupied and by Christmas 1944 Budapest is encircled, holding out until mid-February 1945. In the area of Lake Balaton a German counterattack is launched in March 1945 with the aim of keeping control of the local oil fields.
7. On 12 January 1945 the Red Army launches its major offensive towards Germany; by 31 January, the Soviet 1st and 2nd Bielorussian Fronts have reached the Oder at Frankfurt – about 60km (37 miles) from Berlin. The wedge is widened first to the south, along the Oder and Neisse rivers, then to the north; here, after the failed German counterattack east of Königsberg of 16–20 February 1945, the Red Army sweeps north cutting off Heeresgruppe Nord and establishing a front line along the Oder up to Stettin.

Soviet offensive against Heeresgruppen A and Mitte began on 13 January, the spectre of collapse became reality. On 15 January, as Hitler moved back to Berlin for the last time, Guderian urged him to 'throw everything east'. Hitler then ordered the transfer of some of the units that had been fighting in the Ardennes to Heeresgruppe Süd in Hungary, with the idea of keeping control of the Hungarian oil fields. On 16 January Hitler took direct control over operations on the Eastern Front, and one of his first decisions was to appoint SS leader Heinrich Himmler as commander of the newly formed Heeresgruppe Vistula and organizer of the national defence in the rear areas. The last German offensives on the Eastern Front were complete failures. The relief of Budapest started on 1 January 1945 and made good initial progress, inspiring Guderian to transform it into a major offensive. However, this attack had failed by the end of the month. In March the troops from the Ardennes front arrived and were thrown onto the offensive in the Lake Balaton area, with 6. SS-Panzerarmee leading the way.

This thwarted Guderian's attempts to have 6. SS-Panzerarmee launch an offensive against the Soviet forces now threatening Berlin from the east, timed to coincide with another offensive launched from Stargard in Pomerania. This was now the main German effort to delay the Soviet forces approaching Berlin, placed in Himmler's less-than-capable hands. After waiting for ten days for Himmler to assemble the forces required, on 13 February Guderian managed to have his deputy, General Walther Wenck, put in charge of the offensive. The first attack, by only a single division, was launched on the 15th followed by a general offensive by 11. SS-Panzerarmee the following day. After three days, and an advance of no more than 5km (3 miles), the offensive was halted. Ten days later Guderian was told by the commander of Heeresgruppe Süd that his soldiers were no longer willing to fight;

An infantry assault team climbing onto a Panther tank in Normandy, June 1944. Several Panther battalions still undergoing training were thrown into the battles in north-west Europe to try and stem the Allied advance, thus thwarting Guderian's last efforts to rebuild a core of fully combat-effective Panzer divisions. (Private collection)

German soldiers inspecting an overturned T-34, which has probably fallen from the damaged bridge. With its heavy sloped armour and 76mm gun it outmatched all the German tanks of 1941–42, which were only able to destroy it by firing at very close range (100m or less) at a weak spot to its rear. (Carlo Pecchi)

the war was lost, and everybody knew it. There still was time for small victories, and Guderian had his last on 20 March when he managed to persuade Hitler to remove Himmler from command of Heeresgruppe Vistula and replace him with General Heinrici. Seven days later Guderian had his last clash with Hitler over the failed attempt to relieve Küstrin, on the Oder, through a counterattack. He was given six weeks of sick leave, and Hitler replaced him with General Hans Krebs. The following day Guderian left the OKH staff to join the staff of his other command, that of Generalinspekteur der Panzertruppen. As such he surrendered himself to the US Army on 10 May, two days after the official German surrender.

OPPOSING COMMANDERS

Although German armoured warfare, including the development of the Panzerwaffe, has been amongst the most studied aspects of military history, Germany was by no means the pioneer or foremost proponent of armoured warfare or tank development. That honour falls to Great Britain, who first developed the tank during World War I, with France following closely behind – German efforts lagged behind. The interwar years saw many technical and theoretical developments in the field of armoured warfare, and it was the application of these theories by the German Army during the early years of World War II that has led to many of the myths developing around Heinz Guderian's true abilities. Although he was one of, but far from the only, pioneers of armoured warfare in Germany, much of the doctrine he was applying came from other sources, notably one of the leading theoreticians of armoured warfare, the British officer John Frederick Charles Fuller.

Born in September 1878 in West Sussex and commissioned from Sandhurst in 1899, he attended Staff College at Camberley in 1913. During World War I he served in France as a staff officer and was attached to the heavy branch of the Machine Gun Corps, which eventually became the Tank Corps. He was involved in the planning of the tank attack at Cambrai in 1917 and also for the final offensive of autumn 1918. It was at this early stage that he developed the first real armoured warfare doctrine, 'Plan 1919'. Based on his experiences, Fuller theorized that infantry could not force a real breakthrough of enemy lines, firstly because of their slow pace of advance and secondly because the momentum of their attacks tended to dissipate once the enemy's main line of resistance had been broken. Fuller saw the tank as the solution to these immediate problems, and also developed ideas about their use as a truly decisive weapon.

Thanks to their armour, firepower and mobility, tanks were able to withstand enemy fire while approaching the defences, overcoming them and rupturing the front. Fuller's proposal was for an army entirely made of tanks that, after the breakthrough, could advance deeply into the enemy lines in order to achieve a penetration of such depth and extent that the enemy could not restore the integrity of its defensive lines, something all too possible following an infantry attack.

This theory, radical as it was back then, completely changed the view of modern warfare. Rather than fighting battles of attrition, largely aimed at wearing the enemy down, or battles fought with the intention of breaking the enemy front in order to gain control of a portion of territory, the new form of warfare envisaged penetration in depth behind enemy lines which, unable to withstand an enemy offensive like the main front line, would fall apart causing the collapse of the entire front. Fuller's theories, which focused on basic principles such as surprise, concentration and mobility, were studied and developed in many countries in the interwar years, France, the Soviet Union and Germany amongst them, and gained even more credibility following World War II.

In the 1920s Fuller's work was joined by that of Basil Henry Liddell Hart, a British officer who had fought on the Western Front during the early years of World War I before ill health, caused by a gas attack, caused him to be appointed Inspector General of Training to the British Armies. Transferred after the war to the Army Educational Corps, he wrote the 1920 edition of the official Infantry Manual. Retiring with the rank of captain in 1927,

A camouflaged Artillerie Panzer Beobachtungswagen III, an armoured artillery observation vehicle based on the Panzer III tank developed in February 1943, in use by armoured self-propelled artillery units, an organic part of the Panzer divisions from that year. (Carlo Pecchi)

Liddell Hart became famous as a war correspondent and a writer, and particularly as a theoretician of warfare deeply involved in studying the problems of mechanization. Enjoying much more widespread appeal and success than Fuller, Liddell Hart theorized that future wars would be dominated by mechanization and airpower. Armies should be fully mechanized and motorized and, led by tanks, should be capable of penetrating enemy defensive lines and delivering the 'decisive blow' to the command, control, and communication systems. Although both Fuller and Liddell Hart shared similar views at a tactical and operational level, their approaches were completely different. Liddell Hart talked about the strategy of the 'indirect approach', where the point of attack is aimed at the weakest spot of the enemy defences with the aim of obtaining a disruptive blow to keep an enemy off balance and uncertain. Mechanization was the best way to achieve such an aim as it provided both speed and flexibility, enabling modern armies to break through the enemy main line of defence and then exploit the success with a strategic penetration in depth – a task that was to be reserved for armoured units moving ahead of the rest of the army.

The Panzer II Ausf. L 'Luchs' was the last version of this tank, a reconnaissance vehicle of which only 100 were produced. In the last years of the war the Panzer divisions lacked a suitable fully tracked, armoured reconnaissance vehicle. (Carlo Pecchi)

A 37mm Pak 35/36 in action. Developed from 1934 it was one of the most technologically advanced of its time, only to prove dramatically outdated in 1940 against the heavily armoured French and British tanks that it could not penetrate, eventually being nicknamed the 'door knocker' by its crews. (Private collection)

It is clear how the theories of Fuller and Liddell Hart resemble the theories developed and put into effect by the German Army. Concentration of forces, surprise attacks against weak points on the enemy line, speed, movement, flexibility and penetration in depth of the enemy lines by armoured formations became very familiar after the German successes of the early years of World War II. The problem for the British officers was that, unlike in Germany where theorists of armoured warfare succeeded in imposing themselves, they did not manage to have their ideas adopted in any systematic way.

In 1926 the British Army established the first mechanized unit in the world, the 'Experimental Mechanised Force' that was the centrepiece of the manoeuvres held in May 1927, and it was intended that Fuller should command it. Yet Fuller managed to be sacked by arguing with the War Office over small details, while Liddell Hart bitterly criticized the whole concept at the root of the EMF. In spite of this the development of armoured formations continued at a steady pace until the mid-1930s. The EMF experience provided the basis for the 'purple book', or the first official handbook on armour entitled *Mechanised and Armoured Formations*. The development of radios also brought an important step forward in the British armoured tactics, and in the summer of 1930 an exercise was held that proved the effectiveness of mechanized units which were able to maintain contact with their HQ while on the battlefield. The following year new exercises were held with an entire provisional tank brigade commanded from the CO's tank; this was a considerable way ahead of where other countries were in the development of armoured warfare. And yet in the period 1935–37 Britain lost its technical and theoretical advantages, with the newly developed German Panzer units overtaking them. There were many reasons for this: the effects of the Great Depression, the influence of pacifist movements (of no consequence at all in Germany), the decision to shift the limited public spending to other sectors of the armed forces. There was also another factor: the theorists of armoured warfare were having a hard time and had lost much of their influence.

A destroyed French Char B1 bis heavy tank, May 1940. These were used at Stonne to counterattack Guderian's breakthrough at Sedan and proved invulnerable to the standard 37mm anti-tank gun. The Germans destroyed them using either heavy artillery or anti-aircraft guns. (Carlo Pecchi)

A French Hotchkiss 39 light tank pressed into German service as the Panzer 39H (f). A large number of Panzer units were equipped with captured tanks, mostly employed in training roles but also used for rear-area security and against partisans in the Balkans. (Carlo Pecchi)

Fuller retired from the army in 1933, while Liddell Hart turned his attention to aerial warfare and, from 1932, argued that strategic air power would play the decisive role in future wars and that Britain should rely on maritime and aerial strategies, avoiding any involvement of land forces in a continental war. Given the experiences of the Spanish Civil War, Liddell Hart came to the conclusion that developments in anti-tank weapons had greatly diminished the actual impact of the tank on the battlefield. As he saw it, only fast-moving light tanks were now suitable for combat. There was clearly a great deal of uncertainty on the matter, which contributed to the creation of a tank force made of a mixture of light, fast-moving tanks (for the cavalry units), and slow, heavy armoured 'Infantry' tanks (intended as support), along with that of the faster 'Cruiser' tank for use in manoeuvre operations. In 1931 the British Army created the provisional 1st Tank Brigade, a permanent formation from 1934 and expanded into the Mobile Division in 1938; this became the Armoured Division in 1939. Along with a Tank Brigade this was the only armoured formation of the British Army in 1940, apart from the Mobile Force (Egypt) – later 7th Armoured Division. This was created in 1938 by one of the real pioneers of British tank warfare, Sir Percy Cleghorn Stanley 'Hobo' Hobart. Born in 1885 in India, he studied history, art and literature before entering the Royal Military Academy at Woolwich and being commissioned as an officer of the Royal Corps of Engineers. In 1923, influenced by the writings of Liddell Hart, he volunteered for transfer into the Royal Tank Corps and, following promotion to brigadier in 1934, took over command of the 1st Tank Brigade and became Inspector of the Royal Tank Corps. The situation confronting him was greatly different than that of his German counterpart, Guderian, mainly owing to the lack of financial resources. In 1937 Hobart first became Deputy Director of Staff Duties with a special appointment on AFVs, then Director of Military Training. Promoted major-general, in 1938 he was sent to Egypt with the task of creating what became the 'Mobile Force' and which would provide the core of O'Connor's forces that over a few months in the winter of 1940–41 conquered Cyrenaica and destroyed an Italian army. It is noteworthy that 'Hobo', who, against strong opposition from local commanders, had created this unit, was no longer in charge of it, having been forced into retirement in 1940 by the Commander-in-Chief Middle East Archibald Wavell. Hobart joined the Home Guard as a lance corporal before being recalled to duty in 1941, mainly thanks to the personal intervention of Winston Churchill. Although he never led an armoured unit on the battlefield, Hobart was an able commander who personally created and trained two of the best British armoured divisions of the war: the 11th Armoured Division, which was sent to Tunisia in 1943 and then fought in

A Panzer regiment on field exercises, summer 1939. In the foreground is a Panzer I light tank, ahead of it a light Panzer II armed with a 20mm gun. To the left, in the background, are a Panzer III and Panzer IV medium tank, the first armed with a 37mm gun and the latter with a short-barrelled 75mm. (Private collection)

north-west Europe; and the 79th Armoured Division, a special Royal Engineers unit that developed special tanks and AFVs ('Hobart's Funnies') used with great success during D-Day and throughout North-west Europe.

The British theorists of armoured warfare were, unlike the Germans, never in a position to influence the development of mechanized units or doctrine decisively, though traces of their influence still existed in 1940. Fuller, Liddell Hart and Hobart were all devoted to the concept of the 'tank heavy' armoured division – one almost exclusively made of tank units. So a British armoured division had a comparable number of tanks to a German Panzer division, but it lacked the supporting infantry, artillery and other arms that made the Panzer division a self-contained combat force, fully capable of operating on its own. This was, more or less, the same situation in the French armoured and mechanized forces prior to 1940. Having suffered heavy casualties during World War I, the French Army, once obsessed by the concept of the offence at all costs, reverted to a defensive posture based around both static and flexible defences. Despite this, France built more and better tanks – at least with better armour protection and guns – than any other country apart from the Soviet Union. However, they never developed a doctrine for modern mechanized warfare. The only theorist was Charles de Gaulle. Born in Lille in November 1890 he entered the army in 1909 as an officer cadet and served with distinction during World War I, being wounded three times and taken prisoner in 1916. The interwar French Army was very much controlled from the top down,

A Sturmgeschütz III Ausf. G on the Eastern Front. The first variant of the StuG III armed with the 75mm L/43 or L/48 long barrelled gun was produced from March 1942, but the new version of this assault gun only entered mass production at the end of the year with more than 7,700 built up to March 1945. (Private collection)

Brand new early Tiger I tanks training somewhere in France. Produced from July 1942, the first Tiger-equipped unit was hastily thrown into battle on the Eastern Front in August 1943. Although successful in defence, the Tiger tanks were too heavy and hard to manoeuvre to be useful for long-range offensives. (Private collection)

and its commander-in-chief in the late 1930s, Maurice Gamelin, was the sole arbiter of military doctrine, and there was simply no space for a de Gaulle. His books *Le Fil de l'epée* (*The Edge of the Sword*, 1932) and, particularly, *Vers l'armée de metier* (*Towards a Professional Army*, 1934), advocating the creation of a career army mainly composed of mobile, mechanized forces suitable for rapid offensive operations, had some support from within the army itself, but were criticized both by the army establishment, who were still tied to the horse, and by politicians who feared an attempt to take over the army. In spite of the political protection given to him by Paul Reynaud, de Gaulle's career before the war was unimpressive and, after becoming a tank regiment commander in 1937, in 1939 he commanded the armoured units in the 5e Armée. Only after Reynaud's rise to power in March 1940 de Gaulle was given command of the latest 4e Division blindée, still in the process of being formed.

The difference between German Panzer formations and the French ones was remarkable; the latter had, apart from seven motorized infantry divisions, a mixture of three light mechanized ones (including a cavalry brigade and a mechanized brigade) plus four armoured divisions. These first formed only in January 1940, with the third composed in March and the fourth still forming in May 1940. It is important to point out that, despite all the shortcomings that handicapped the impact of the French armour during the 1940 campaign, it could still be effective under a skilled and determined leadership. De Gaulle's counterattacks against Guderian's drive from Sedan on 17–20 May were considered by German officers to be the best and most dangerous they experienced during the campaign. De Gaulle fought another action at Abbeville on 28–30 May, before being promoted brigadier-general on 1 June and eventually joining Reynaud's government five days later as undersecretary for the national defence, a post he only held for ten days before Reynaud's resignation. Brought to Britain in an RAF aircraft, his career as a leader of the Free French and, later, as President of the French Republic, is well known.

Just like Britain, the Soviet Union was an early starter in the development of theories on mechanized warfare, their basic concept being that of the 'deep battle'. Developed out of the experiences of World War I, this was based on the notion that once the crust of an enemy's defensive position had been broken, then aircraft and mechanized forces had to be used to expand the breakthrough and conduct deep operations into the enemy's rear, not allowing him the opportunity of re-establishing his defensive line. First developed between 1929 and 1935, the operational concept was refined in 1936 as 'deep operation', consisting of a series of penetration and exploitation movements as deep as 100km (62 miles) behind the enemy front line to prevent the establishment of a firm line of defence. The man behind these theories was General, from 1936 Marshal, Mikhail Nikolayevich Tukhachevsky. Born in February 1893 to an aristocratic family, he graduated from the Alexsandrovskoye Military School in 1914. He served during World War I as a second lieutenant until his capture in 1915 (as a POW he met Charles de Gaulle), only to escape successfully in 1917 and eventually join the Bolsheviks during the Civil War. He led the Red Army in the war against Poland, during which he had his first clash with Stalin, and was defeated. Despite this, from 1925 to 1928 he was chief of staff and deputy commissar for defence, and undertook a major reorganization of the Red Army and developed the 'deep battle' and 'deep operation' theory.

Fuller, Liddell Hart and Guderian

In the German edition of his memoirs, Guderian writes how his interest was aroused by the writings of Fuller, Liddell Hart and Martens. However, their actual influence seems to have been minimal, and when Fuller – after his involvement with Oswald Mosley's British Union of Fascists following retirement in 1933 – visited Germany in 1939 on the occasion of Hitler's 50th birthday and watched a military parade of the Panzerwaffe, there was no meeting between him and Guderian. Guderian's contacts with Liddell Hart were post-war, when the latter started his series of interviews with German generals that led to the book *The Other Side of the Hill*. Recent analysis has shown how Liddell Hart attempted to propagate a distorted view of the extent to which his theories were studied and put into effect by the Germans, including having a paragraph added to the English edition of Guderian's memoirs stating how he 'learned from them [Fuller, Liddell Hart and Martens, or 'far-sighted soldiers'] the concentration of armour', and how 'it was Liddell Hart who emphasised the use of armoured forces for long-range strokes, operations against the opposing army's communications, and also proposed a type of armoured division combining Panzer and Panzer-infantry units', concluding 'So I owe many suggestions of our further development to Captain Liddell Hart' (*Panzer Leader*, page 20). Liddell Hart's letter to Guderian, in which he asked for the importance of his theories to be stressed, was found by Kenneth Macksey amongst Guderian's papers. Liddell Hart, when questioned on the matter in 1968, did not deny it and it also illustrates how Guderian was inclined to rewrite history in his memoirs.

Shortly after his promotion to marshal, Stalin had Tukhachevsky and seven other high-ranking officers arrested, put on trial secretly and executed in June 1937. His writings banned, no space was left for the development of mechanized warfare in the Red Army. So, even though the first two Soviet mechanized corps were formed as early as 1932, and had a balanced combined-arms organization, once the purges started the quality declined. Amongst those who survived the purges was General, later Marshal, Georgy Konstantinovich Zhukov, born in December 1896 to a poor family and conscripted in the army in 1915. He joined the Bolsheviks after the 1917 revolution and fought in the Civil War, and in 1930 was given command of a brigade. His survival during Stalin's purges was probably helped by his connection to Marshal Semyon Budyonny, one of only two of this rank to survive. In 1939, as commander of 1st Army Group in Mongolia, he fought against the Japanese successfully in the battle of Khalkhin Gol, the first battlefield test of the 'deep operation' theory. In January 1941 he became chief of army staff and deputy commissar of defence, and during the war he was the mainspring of Soviet strategy and operations.

A mixed group of infantry and Panzers advancing on the Eastern Front. The tanks include light Panzer II and Czech-produced Panzer 35 (t) tanks. Incorporated after the annexation of Czechoslovakia, some 1,400 Czech Panzer 35 and 38s were used by the German Army, mostly Panzer 38s which were produced until June 1942. (Private collection)

WHEN WAR IS DONE

After his capture by the Americans on 10 May 1945, Guderian managed to avoid being handed over to the Soviets, despite official requests, and instead became part of the US Army Historical Division's 'Foreign Military Studies Program', started in 1945, fully developed from 1948 and brought to an end in 1954. Guderian's activity seems to have been quite limited, since he only wrote four small 'studies' himself and collaborated in the writing of three others. This is probably due to his early release from captivity on 16 June 1948, sooner than other German generals and having avoided being tried for his activities as either a field commander or chief of the army staff

(Erich von Manstein was sentenced in 1949 by a British tribunal to 18 years, eventually released in 1953; Alfred Kesselring was sentenced to life in 1947, released in 1952, to mention just two prominent generals). In June 1950 Guderian retired with his wife to a small house in Schwangau by Füssen and began writing. His first book, published in 1950, was a clear attempt to highlight the need for Germany's rearming, and was aptly entitled *Kann Westeuropa verteidigt werden?* (*Can Western Europe be Defended?*). In the same year his *Erinnerungen* were also published, followed in 1952 by a very successful English translation. Other works written by Guderian before his death in May 1954 dealt with historical subjects, mainly concerning the 1940 campaign. His eldest son Heinz Günther started his military career in 1933 and, having served in Panzer-Regimenter 1 and 35, entered the War Academy in 1942 and became the operation officer of 116. Panzer-Division in 1944 (also winning the Knight's Cross in October). In the post-war Bundeswehr he followed in his father's footsteps by commanding a Panzer battalion and a regiment before joining the army staff and ending up as Generalinspekteur das Panzertruppen before his retirement in 1974.

INSIDE THE MIND

Heinz Guderian was an undoubtedly ambitious, innovative, energetic and self-centred individual whose ego was, at least at first, equalled by the results he was able to achieve, and subsequently fed by worldwide admiration. Although part of the German military elite, he stood at its very fringes until his career as a pioneer of the Panzerwaffe began. However, he was not a maverick officer in the style of Rommel, as he preferred the semi-obscure environment of the general staff to the glittering role of the 'star' of the German Panzer forces. A position he could have achieved had he been willing, like Rommel, to be a kind of 'media star' but, as he told his wife, this was not what he wanted, but rather what he loathed. However, what he did have in common with Rommel and others of his ilk was his attitude to National Socialism and Hitler, which gave his career a much-needed boost.

Despite his background and early career, Guderian was not really a full member of the German military elite, and this was partly due to his technical background. However, this background proved useful in the interwar German Army when

A formal portrait of Heinz Guderian on the Eastern Front in summer 1941, after he had been awarded the Eichenlaub to his Ritterkreuz. The encirclement of Kiev that summer was the pinnacle of his military successes. (Nik Cornish, WH 804)

Guderian, as Generalinspekteur der Panzertruppen, reviews Panzer-Regiment 'Grossdeutschland'. Behind him stands its commander, Oberst Graf Hyazinth Strachwitz von Gross-Zauche und Camminetz. Although officially a Panzergrenadier division, by July 1944 the 'Grossdeutschland' included (on paper at least) a three-battalion Panzer regiment. (Private collection)

it was acknowledged that technological innovation was seen as the means by which the stalemate of World War I could be avoided. His developments in the fields of armoured and mechanized warfare were considered innovative and progressive, especially in the conservative environment of the German general staff, despite not being particularly original. Guderian's rise came through a lucky combination of his personal ambition and drive, and the situation of Germany and her armed forces during the interwar period. This enabled him to reach positions where his ideas were not only accepted, but also put into practice. He did face opposition, but never to the extent of the 'tank prophets' outside Germany. He could always rely on support from influential superiors, whose trust he was able to gain.

His ambition and his energy filled the gap between the staff officer more used to theories and paperwork and the field officer, who had to face different challenges. Guderian proved a capable field commander, who had good leadership skills and performed his tasks in close accordance with the basic requirements of the German army. His continuous 'leading from the front' was, in fact, nothing more than what the German officers were simply asked to do; he may have been stubborn, ruthless, and even arrogant when dealing with the enemy and his own subordinates, but these were the characteristics that all too often made a good leader and commander. He was not flawless, however, and failed to appreciate the differences between the 1940 campaign against France and the 1941 one against the Soviet Union. If in the former taking risks, such as splitting his forces in a decisive manoeuvre, gave positive results, in the latter it turned into an unnecessary dispersion and attrition of his forces. The common attitude among German commanders of not bothering overly about logistics seems to have been more accentuated in Guderian who, even after his experiences during the Anschluß with Austria, proved careless about the attrition rate of his Panzer and the subsequent loss of fighting power of his forces. His irascibility (which also earned him the nickname 'Heinz Brausewetter', 'Heinz stormy weather') and insistence on turning every clash into a personal quarrel turned adversaries into enemies, such as Kluge.

Guderian's self-centred ego and his failure to assess properly the lessons of the early blitzkrieg seems to have been the origin of a certain detachment from reality. If in early 1943 his reorganization plan, as Generalinspekteur das Panzertruppen, still made sense, it should have become clear from the end of 1943 and the beginning of 1944 that it was a failure. Nevertheless, Guderian failed to develop an alternative plan to restore efficiency of the Panzer forces. Facing the challenges of strategic decisions under difficult circumstances, the innovative Guderian proved unable to conceive new ideas, and got bogged down by simple, straightforward decisions. This can be seen clearly in his experiences as chief of the army staff, when his 'hold every inch of ground' attitude seems to have been inspired both by his personal desire to keep the war away from his native East Prussia and to a certain acquiescence to Hitler's own strategy.

His attitude toward National Socialism does not appear to have differed greatly from that of the average German, particularly those of the military elite. After Hitler's rise to power in 1933 Guderian enjoyed the advantages offered by the new regime. He developed close relationships with Nazi Party personalities, like the leader of the National Socialist Motor Corps (NSKK) Adolf Hühnlein, and came to be very close to Hitler himself. While boosting his career, this also seems to have exacerbated Guderian's critical attitude towards the old school of the German officers whom he repeatedly criticized. Following the July 1944 plot against Hitler, Guderian was not only part of the honour court that dismissed officers involved before sending them for trial, but he also advocated strongly that army staff personnel needed to be 'good National Socialists'. However, in the critical days at the end of the

Hitler at his conference table surrounded by his generals. From left to right Alfred Jodl, chief of staff of the Oberkommando der Wehrmacht (OKW), Franz Halder chief of the army staff, Hitler, General Walther von Brauchitsch, chief of the army, and behind him Field Marshal Wilhelm Keitel, chief of the general staff (OKW). Although taken in July 1940, the photo gives an idea of how Hitler worked along with his military entourage. (IWM, HU 75533)

Third Reich, Guderian chose not to remain with his Führer, and instead fled to a part of Germany far away from the threat of the Red Army.

Guderian's realistic attitude was also prominent in the post-war years, as his relationship with Liddell Hart shows. By skilfully portraying himself as the 'father' of the Panzertruppen, he not only managed to avoid consignment into Soviet hands, but also carved a niche for himself in the American-sponsored 'history writing' project that granted him release from captivity without trial. In fact Guderian's biggest rewriting of history is not so much the one about his 'fatherhood' of the Panzertruppen, but rather his lack of any involvement in war crimes during Operation *Barbarossa*. Units of his *Panzergruppe* received and implemented the 'commissar order' authorizing summary execution, while in his position of chief of army staff he had a prominent role in the reprisal against the Warsaw uprising in summer 1944.

A LIFE IN WORDS

Heinz Guderian's personal literary success has caused many problems with assessing his reputation. Like many other World War II German generals, Guderian's stock has risen and fallen over the years. Exaggerated praise has been followed by more nuanced reflections, until in recent years his conduct and career has been criticised, sometimes harshly. The discovery of new sources and studies has led to reassessments and re-evaluation of many aspects of the history of World War II. Yet with Guderian it appears sometimes as if the whole of his career and his achievements have been downplayed and devalued.

The problems begin with Guderian's own memoirs. Lacking other sources, and given their success, historians used them as a source for quite a long

Three days after its award on 27 October 1939, Guderian is presented by Hitler with the Ritterkreuz which he earned as commander of XIX AK (mot.) during the Polish campaign. To his right, in the foreground, is General Franz Halder, chief of the army staff.
(Private collection)

time, even well after other documents had become available. It is difficult to blame Guderian for having written a book of memoirs that is self-centred, like all memoirs, uncritical of his own role and prone to exaggeration when it comes to his part in affairs. Instead, historians should be criticized for relying so much on this one single publication, and for the fact that we still do not have one fully researched, archive-driven biography of Guderian, or even an in-depth analysis of the role and the evolution of the German Panzer forces during the war. This makes any balanced analysis or assessment a difficult task.

In looking at Guderian away from his literary skills and fortunes, he comes across as a career officer who developed an interest in technical developments at a time when these were being examined by other people, in Germany as well as elsewhere. Guderian was one of the innovators, not the only one and, above all, not the 'father' of the Panzertruppen. And yet, Guderian possessed genuine skills and talent; he was able to turn this interest of his into a vocation, eventually having his voice heard at the highest levels. This talent for innovation was matched with ambition and other skills that helped his career, something that many other innovators lacked. Even though he was not the first, and probably not even the most prominent, advocate of tanks and mechanized warfare, Guderian succeeded in carving a role (and a career) for himself and in taking full advantage of the opportunities he was given, both by his immediate superiors and by the political establishment. Although it is possible to debate forever whether it was Lutz or Guderian who actually instigated the development of the Panzer forces, what is not up for debate is that it was Guderian who stood in the limelight – almost certainly with Lutz's approval – at a time when the German armoured and mechanized units were still in their infancy.

Guderian's SdKfz 251/6 command vehicle stops to permit the commander to discuss the situation with one of his subordinates during the campaign in the west in May 1940. With its radio equipment (hence the large frame antennae), this command vehicle enabled Guderian to reach his spearhead units while keeping in touch with his HQ. (Private collection)

If Guderian's 'fatherhood' of the Panzertruppen can be criticized, the role he played in the decisive years right before and immediately after the outbreak of World War II must be acknowledged. Between 1938 and 1940 Guderian supervised and then tested on the battleground those Panzer divisions that, to a large extent, were his creation. He rightly understood the need for a combined-arms and balanced unit, and the effect that attrition would play on the Panzers while in action. Guderian's role in the development of the actual organization of the Panzer divisions is unquestionable; he was the one that made them an instrument of warfare capable of carrying out an independent role. His attention to such technical matters as communications, supply, and maintenance made it possible for Guderian to adapt modern mechanized warfare to the older, well-established tactical and operational concepts already in use in the German Army. His motto of 'strike concentrated, not dispersed' was not an innovation per se, as concepts like concentration of forces, selection of a focal point, etc., were a reality well before the age of the Panzer. Guderian's real innovative contribution was the adaption of modern technical innovations to these concepts and, above all, his actual first-hand proving of the concept on the battlefield as a commander.

Guderian had remarkable command and leadership skills, so often missing from great theoreticians, though he was sometimes helped by good luck and also made mistakes. The most remarkable of these was his failure to appreciate the real circumstances that led to the victory against France in 1940, and his inability to adapt to the changing situation faced on the Eastern Front. Guderian's lack of flexibility is the other side of the coin of his innovative spirit. This accounts for the eventual failure he met as Generalinspekteur der Panzertruppen, first, when he proved unable to react to the needs of the moment while implementing his reorganization plan,

An early Panther Ausf. A on the Eastern Front in 1943. Cheaper than the Tiger I (each Panther cost, 117,000 Marks in comparison to 250,000 for a Tiger), 1,848 were produced in 1943 followed by 3,777 in 1944 but only 507 in 1945. On 1 March 1945 the German Army had 1,964 of them, plus 189 with the home army. (Private collection)

A column of late-production Tiger Is on the Eastern Front. Even though its crews considered it invulnerable, Guderian noted in October 1943 that it could be destroyed by the Soviet 76.2mm gun at a range of 500m, while its bulk attracted massive enemy fire, even from the artillery. (Private collection)

and then as Chef des Stabes des OKH. In this role Guderian would revert to a 'classic' form of high-level generalship, proving excessively prone to Hitler's own strategy and reluctant to embrace any kind of 'innovative' idea, whether a major redeployment of forces on the Eastern Front or the Ardennes counteroffensive.

His adaptability and drive would help him once more in the post-war years, when he was able to first avoid any kind of trouble as a prisoner of war, and then when he started the creation of his own myth, something he only achieved with the helpful assistance of writers such as Liddell Hart and the many other historians that followed. Another reason was the need to create a different image of the German generals and of their armies. As the war now belonged to history, and NATO needed to rebuild Germany's military to face the Soviet threat, the need for new perspectives on the former enemy eventually prevailed. From this point of view, Guderian fits perfectly the image of the professional, imaginative and skilled soldier who perfectly knew the dangers of the threats from the east, and the creation of

A Sturmgeschütz III of a Waffen-SS unit heavily laden with soldiers. The side skirts, or Schürzen, mounted on German tanks from 1943, were intended to reduce the effectiveness of enemy hollow-charge shells

his myth also served the purpose of creating the myth of a German Army not fully tainted by Hitler's madness. As Liddell Hart wrote in the introduction to *Panzer Leader*:

> Guderian was a single-minded soldier, professional in the truest sense – the quintessence of the craftsman in the way he devoted himself to the progress of a technique.... There one can find a natural explanation of his attitude toward Hitler – clearly more favourable than that of most of the generals brought up in the old tradition. Hitler manifested a liking for new military ideas, and for the tank idea in particular, so Guderian was naturally disposed to like him. Hitler showed an inclination to back that revolutionary idea, so Guderian was inclined to back him. Hitler was in conflict with the General Staff and with established conventions; so was Guderian in this sphere.

It is no coincidence that many of the German generals serving time in prison were in fact released in the early 1950s, but Guderian's myth would prove to be a long-lasting one. For example, in 1973 John Keegan wrote in his more balanced Ballantine biography of Guderian that he 'never swerved from his belief in the battle-winning power of armour-air formations, as Liddell Hart did in the years before the Second World War.... Indeed, he was his own man his whole life. It was that, and his single-minded determination to restore the military reputation of the German army which make him one of the most memorable of all its officers.'

FURTHER READING

Anyone interested in Heinz Guderian's life and activities should start with his own works; his first book, published in Berlin in 1937, was entitled *Die Panzertruppen und ihr Zusammenwirken mit den anderen Waffen* (*The Panzertruppen and their cooperation with other arms*), translated and published in English in 2003 by the Naval & Military Press. His renowned *Achtung – Panzer!*, published in 1937 in Stuttgart, has recently been translated and published in English as well (*Achtung – Panzer! The Development of Armoured Forces, their Tactics and Operational Potential*, translated by Christopher Duffy and edited by Paul Harris; London: Arms and Armour Press, 1992). Guderian's post-war memoirs, *Erinnerungen eines Soldaten* (*Memoirs of a Soldier*), was first published in Heidelberg by Kurt Vowinckel in 1950, and translated and published in English in 1952 with an introduction by B. H. Liddell Hart under the title *Panzer Leader*. It has had several subsequent editions in both languages. Practically every single biographer of Guderian, either supportive or critical, has heavily relied on these. The first biography of Heinz Guderian actually appeared before his death: Malte Plattenberg, *Guderian. Hintergrunde des deutschen Schicksal 1918–1945* (Düsseldorf, 1950). The first English-language biography is by John Keegan in the Ballantine series, *Guderian* (New York, 1973), followed two years later by the first of Kenneth Macksey's two books he wrote on him, *Guderian: Panzer General* (London, 1975), and the more thorough and balanced *Guderian: Creator of the Blitzkrieg* (New York, 1976). In 1978 two other biographies were published in Germany, Karl J. Walde's *Guderian* (Frankfurt/Main, Berlin, Wien), and Günter Fraschka's *Generaloberst Heinz Guderian. Der kühnste Panzerführer des letzten Krieges* (Rastatt). By the mid-1980s two more biographies were published in Germany, apparently making Guderian the most popular general of the war (in Germany, at least): Fred Frank's *Heinz Guderian. Der geniale Panzerführer des II. Weltkrieges* (Rastatt, 1985; reprinted in 2006 with the title: *Heinz Guderian: zwischen Genialität und Legende. Der soldatische Lebensweg der des berühmtesten deutschen Panzergenerals*), and Dermot Bradley's *Generaloberst Heinz Guderian und die Entstehunggeschichte des modernen Blitzkrieges* (Osnabrück, 1986), so far the most scholarly work to have been published, even if mostly limited to Guderian's role in the pre-war development of the Panzerwaffe. Guderian's most recent biography, published 20 years after the last, is also the most critical of both his life and works: Russell Hart's *Guderian: Panzer Pioneer or Myth Maker* (Washington, DC, 2006) has the advantage of having been written after the end of the Cold War and Germany's reunification, therefore his critical analysis is free from any of the restraint of the past. However, Hart is excessively critical of Guderian, which makes his book appear more like an attempt to destroy the man and his story than a balanced account. He also largely relies on Guderian's *Erinnerungen* rather than on new records, as does Hans-Heinrich Wilhelm in his (still unpublished) new biography of Guderian in German (see his essay 'Heinz Guderian - »Panzerpapst« und Generalstabschef', in *Die Militärelite des Dritten Reiches*, edited by Ronald Smelser and Enrico Syring, Berlin: Ullstein, 1995)

INDEX